Dearest Kim,

Appreciate i

Know That

you are enough :-)

5/5/18

"In this raw and honest read, Dr. Deering shows a proven path for reaping great rewards in mother–daughter relationships. Prepare to experience more fulfillment."

Kary Oberbrunner, author of
Your Secret Name and *Elixir Project*

"Mothers and daughters *can* "get" each other again as they address where they've "miss"-ed it. In *What Mothers Never Tell Their Daughters*, Michelle shows readers how to fix interpersonal rifts and experience healing in their mother-daughter relationship."

Dr. Jen Welter, First Female NFL coach,
Author of *Play Big*, Advisory Board Member
for the Pro Football Hall of Fame's A Game
for Life Academy, Motivational Speaker

"Dr. Michelle Deering's new book, *What Mother's Never Tell Their Daughters*, is the perfect combination of wit, charm, insight, compassion, education, practical how-tos, healing, and spirit! She uses her personal experiences and wisdom as a daughter, mother, and psychologist in a way that will inspire, nurture, and celebrate the fullness of what it means to be a woman, despite our imperfections and struggles! This is a must-read for mothers and daughters of all ages, from all walks of life.

Denise Johnson, Ph.D., Radio Host of *Spiritual Principles for Emotional Healing*, wdjyfm.com,
Licensed Psychologist, West Orange, New Jersey

"*What Mothers Never Tell Their Daughters* is a timely book that helps mothers and daughters see each other more clearly and connect with each other more meaningfully. Dr. Deering's 5-step process takes readers on a journey towards healing."

Jim D. Akers, Author of Amazon #1
New Release *Tape Breakers: Maximize Your
Impact with People You Love, Teams You
Lead and Causes that Stir Your Heart*

"*What Mothers Never Tell Their Daughters* is an incredibly important book for these times. Dr. Deering has organized her perspectives as daughter, mother, and psychologist in a format that makes the read riveting. The flow kept this reader very involved and, all the while, thinking of friends, colleagues, and patients who would relate to the author's journey and benefit from her gleaned wisdom."

Sheila S. Bender, PhD, Licensed Psychologist, Approved Consultant in EMDR, Author of *The Energy of Belief: Psychology's Power Tools to Focus Intentions and Release Blocking Beliefs*

WHAT MOTHERS
Never Tell
THEIR DAUGHTERS

WHAT MOTHERS *Never Tell* THEIR DAUGHTERS

5 KEYS TO BUILDING TRUST, RESTORING CONNECTION, AND STRENGTHENING RELATIONSHIPS

DR. MICHELLE DEERING

Printed in the United States of America

Published by Author Academy Elite
P.O. Box 43, Powell, OH 43035

www.AuthorAcademyElite.com

The Life Mirror Remedy and the Five Keys (Face It, Clarify It, Spray It, Cover It, and Engage It) are registered service marks of Dr. Michelle T. Deering. All rights reserved.

All Scripture quotations, unless otherwise indicated, are taken from the Holy Bible, New International Version®, NIV®. Copyright ©1973, 1978, 1984, 2011 by Biblica, Inc.™ Used by permission of Zondervan. All rights reserved worldwide. www.zondervan.com The "NIV" and "New International Version" are trademarks registered in the United States Patent and Trademark Office by Biblica, Inc.™

Paperback ISBN: 978-1-64085-235-8

Hardcover ISBN: 978-1-64085-236-5

Ebook ISBN: 978-1-64085-237-2

Library of Congress Control Number: 2018934775

DEDICATION

To my Trojan.
I get it now.
Thank you.
Luv,
Mich

TABLE OF CONTENTS

INTRODUCTION xiii

SECTION 1: THE RIFTS

Part 1: Miss Conceptions: Mirror, Mirror on the Wall

Chapter 1—(Un)Fairness of Life 5

Chapter 2—Fairness of Life. 13

Chapter 3—Who's the Fairest One of All? 23

Part 2: Miss Understandings: Reflection or Not

Chapter 4—Distortion Away! 33

Chapter 5—Whudchisee 43

Chapter 6— . . . Izwhudchaget 51

Part 3: Miss Communications: Cracked Lenses

Chapter 7—Busted Protections 65

Chapter 8—Busted Expectations 75

Chapter 9—Busted Relations 85

SECTION 2: THE REMEDY

Part 4: The Fix: First Four Keys

Chapter 10—Face It 97

Chapter 11—Clarify It 111

Chapter 12—Spray It 117

Chapter 13—Cover It 133

Part 5: Engage It: The Fifth Key

Chapter 14—For Daughter's Sake 153

Chapter 15—For Mother's Sake 165

SECTION 3: THE REWARD

Chapter 16—The TriFecta Rewards 183

EPILOGUE: THE LETTERS

Letter to My BFF Hubby 195

Letter to My Daughters 197

Letter to Single Moms 203

TABLE OF CONTENTS

Acknowledgements 205

Appendix 207

Endnotes 211

About the Author 217

INTRODUCTION

The kitchen was pale aqua green with chips of paint sticking out of the wall. From my room, I heard my name called for dinner. When I arrived, I sat down on a rickety vinyl chair at a 3-foot diameter aluminum table. Her back was to me as she moved slowly from a narrow white gas stove to the dish rack. It had been a long day for both of us.

When my mom turned around, I could see the lines around her plum-shaped cheeks sagging from her long ride on the train and bus from Manhattan's sweatshop in the garment district. After 12 hours of doing piece-work, her shoulders were hunched.

Yet her hands gathered whatever strength remained to carry a plate of food. One plate of food was all there was. On that one plate was one piece of calf liver cooked with a few slivers of onions and the last small remains of a can of green peas scooped next to it. As she got to the table, my mom wearily sat down, the plate immediately landing between us.

For what would seem instantaneous to an outsider but which between the two of us in that moment was an eternity of conversation, she slid the plate of food over to me. I ate it all, knowing that my mom would go hungry that night . . . again.

I was about five years old at the time. I can recall earlier occasions when I would offer my Mom some of the food she'd made, and she would decline, settling for whatever scraps were left from my rejection of certain vegetables. But this particular recollection sticks out in my mind because when our eyes locked, the gentle nodding of her head in my direction (which was her way of letting me know it was okay for me to eat) and my agreeing to eat was our way of acknowledging that we knew that we were in this life *together*. We understood that she was forgoing her hopes and dreams and placing them all on me—a burden no child should ever bear.

Back then, TV advertisements for the food industry propagated the notion that life was so hard for women, and *their* particular products could make it easier for a mother to prepare a quick meal for her family. The offer of a speedy dinner was couched in the promise that moms would then be able to enjoy some personal downtime.

Well, for my mom, nothing was quick. Everything was *long*. Long bus rides, long train rides, long work hours—and then she'd head back home, rinse, and repeat. She did not have time to enjoy herself. She was too busy and too tired.

For my mom that night (and many other nights), life was hard, cooking was hard, and she went to bed hungry.

Isn't that just like a mom? *My* mom. My Trojan—a nickname I'd given her because of my love for the University of Southern California football team's Trojan mascot. I was (and still am) a huge college football fan, and the image of the Trojan riding Traveler the horse around the stadium symbolized strength and victory. This was how I saw my mom: selflessly going out to battle and returning home with food at the end of the day.

As I sit here looking back on that slumlord-run apartment in the South Bronx, I realize that I have a manicured lawn covered with trees and a beautiful new home where I lay my head to rest at the end of my day and go to bed full. Thoughts of my mom fill my mind. It's been 25 years since my husband and I got married. In that time, I've given birth to twin daughters and earned a doctoral degree. A doctor! I'm the only one of my mom's children who became a doctor.

She thought I would be a doctor of medicine, but I got my doctorate in counseling psychology. But I'm jumping ahead of myself . . . more about that in Chapter 8.

For years, I hesitated to write this book. Reflecting on my mom, I thought there was no way I could ever convey or measure up to the example she was for me early in my life. But even as I'd think that, another part of me would realize how much of her example I did not want to emulate. Then feelings of anger (which usually cover up hurt) would well up all over again. I balked at the thought of writing *anything* positive about her. "But she *birthed* me," would be my internal retort about such reflections.

And so the stalemate continued, as did the years of thinking about writing this book.

As my husband and I raised our twin daughters, I often found myself wondering if I was even doing it right—this *mothering* thing. Who was I to write a book about motherhood?

Then, amidst some frustrations I was experiencing with our daughters, my mom came to mind. I had one of *those* moments. Suddenly, what she may have been experiencing or trying to do as a mom made sense.

"But I'm X-years old!" was my next thought. I knew I didn't want my girls to have to wait that many years before they "got" it or "got" me.

So I started thinking about how I could give our girls an understanding about me—their mom. I mulled that idea over and over in my heart for another couple of years. Yup—*more years*.

Then we moved to a new neighborhood and I met many mothers of children under the age of ten. Ahh, the ten-and-under, pre-middle-school age. It was fun to see all the kids, but I felt old, as if I'd been "been there, done that" for that age group. This was a new situation for me. I'd spent my girls' pre-middle-school years thinking, "Is there life after 10?" Now there I was, amongst these young(er) moms and able to say, "*Yesss!* I made it."

As I got to know these incredible mothers, I heard them talk about their experiences with their children. I started to notice a difference in the tone and manner in which they spoke about their daughters in particular. At first, I thought I imagined it. But being naturally curious, I started to wonder about the difference I was noticing.

It seemed that a daughter who exhibited traits similar to her mother's or maternal grandmother's traits would provoke a tone of tension in her mother's voice and body language. No sooner had I made this observation than I began to notice the same tendency in myself. My reactions to my daughters' behaviors, other mom's reactions to their daughters' behaviors—all of it hit me in the face. It was as if a mirror had been placed in front of me and jerked me down memory lane in a nanosecond.

My insides cringed with each mother's tense daughter-related comments as I felt remnants of the pain of my own mom's critical remarks about me. My heart ached for moms and their daughters, and I realized that I wanted to help them relate to one another better.

But then my thoughts would wander to our twin daughters. As I thought about them, I would recall the countless run-ins where, in the aftermath, I've gone back to my truth-telling, ever-patient husband (my BFF hubby), thrown my hands up in the air, and declared, "I'm done! I'm *done* with them!"

Bless his heart, he would simply listen and let me know that I was a great mom and that our girls did not understand all I do for them. "They don't have a context yet," he'd say. His comments and encouragement would calm me down. Then he would tell me his observations about what had transpired between my daughters and me from *their* perspective. In those moments, I'd have my heart tugged with empathy for them, and what I'd contributed to the unhelpful dynamic would become clearer to me.

When our daughters began high school, these moments of clarity began to occur more often. I soon got tired of the cycle—situation, reaction, run-in, blowup, back to separate corners.

I gave myself a hard pause. I could no longer ignore or push aside the reality that I really wanted my daughters and me to have a better understanding of one another. I also wanted them to know that I was learning and trying to understand them better. This got me thinking about how I could help other daughters know that they are understood by a mom (me) in hopes they'd know that their own moms—underneath it all—understand them, but may not yet be able to demonstrate it. I began thinking about how to help daughters help their moms understand them.

Few gifts are greater that the gift of understanding. Communication that ends in understanding helps mothers and daughters connect better.

As a licensed clinical psychologist for nearly 20 years, I've provided therapy to countless female (and male) college students who have told me about their mothers. Though the research literature indicates the significant impact mothers have on a child's development, it wasn't until I began working as an eating disorder (ED) specialist that the M–D (Mother–Daughter) Relationship Dynamics™ (MDRDs) began coming to the forefront of my thinking.

For example, during consultation calls with my ED clients' mothers, I noticed that the degree of tension and unresolved conflict between clients and their moms would manifest itself in the severity of their symptoms. As those tensions got resolved—either within the M–D Relationship interactions or the daughters' responses—the symptoms would dissipate.

For confidentiality reasons, I cannot reference any of the wonderful and brave young collegiate women who've bared their hearts, pain, and tears within my office. But I can say that just as their stories remain with me as a reminder of the privilege I've had to join with and help them on their journey toward healing and wholeness, their stories have also remained with me and helped me in my own mothering.

It is with these three perspectives—as a daughter of a single mom, as a mom of twin teen daughters, and as a clinical psychologist—that I write the following pages. I am humbled and honored that you have chosen to purchase this book and join me on the journey within these pages. It is my hope that you will see with more clarity a reflection of what has been staring at you in your respective mother–daughter relationships.

Similar to the way I work with my clients, I have organized this book into three parts:

Section One (The Rifts) will cover the three main areas in which mothers and daughters "miss" each other—Miss Conceptions, Miss Communications, and Miss Understandings.

Section Two (The Remedy) will guide you through a process of reflection which can be used to facilitate more understanding and give suggestions for improving your M–D Relationship.

Section Three (The Reward) will summarize observations about the whole journey toward closure, closeness, and collaboration in your M–D Relationship.

At or near the end of most chapters, I will offer you four things:

1. **View from the Couch**—my thoughts and heartfelt maternal musings on the chapter's topic

2. **View from the Chair**—my clinical psychologist commentary on the topic

3. **Code Cracker**—a question prompter for you to consider more deeply if you are a mother or daughter reading this book

4. **WMNTTD** (What Mothers Never Tell Their Daughters)—a maternal confession that you can use

as a conversation starter with either your mother or your (16-year-old+) daughter

Know that I am with you on this journey. I have been there as a daughter and a mother on the proverbial couch. I have also been there as one who has helped other young and seasoned ladies while they were on the couch in my office, and they have made great strides in their M–D Relationships. Be encouraged, and let's go crack the code of the mother–daughter relationship . . . *together.*

SECTION ONE
THE RIFTS

We often pass by objects within which we can see our reflection. Some objects give clearer reflections than others. A mirror is the object people usually seek out to see their own reflection. If that mirror is clean, it can show us the most accurate information about ourselves externally while giving us insights into what may be occurring internally.

What we get out of our interaction with a mirror depends on what we focus on when we look at ourselves and what we remember from the encounter after we leave the mirror. You'd be remiss if you looked into a mirror, walked away, and then immediately forgot what you'd seen.

The same can be said for parent–child—in particular, mother–daughter—relationships. Research has shown that a mother's bond with her child is foundational to a child's sense of the world around them and who they are in the world.[1] The interpersonal dynamic of mirroring—reflecting back to a child their facial, tonal, and emotional expressions—is key to a child learning important mental, emotional, and social skills needed for the future development of their sense of who they are as a person. The quality of a daughter's face-to-face time with her mother, the quality of their early attachment, and the way both mother and daughter negotiate physical separation and mental/emotional separateness will impact a daughter's sense of who she is as a girl, young lady, and adult woman.

Poorly navigated instances of differences—the rifts—within the M–D Relationship are equivalent to a mother or daughter looking into a mirror and then forgetting what she saw. Thus, they "miss it" with each other in three areas:

- Conceptions (Chapters 1–3)
- Understandings (Chapters 4–6)
- Communications (Chapters 7–9)

PART 1
MISS CONCEPTIONS
MIRROR, MIRROR ON THE WALL

"Criticism is a misconception:
we must read not to understand others but to
understand ourselves."

—Emile M. Cioran, *Anathemas and Admirations*
Romanian Philosopher

CHAPTER 1
(UN)FAIRNESS OF LIFE

That day she packed up her bags and put on her coat. Then she packed up an eleven-year-old girl's bags and put on her coat and snuck out of an apartment building somewhere in Brooklyn, NY. She walked away not knowing where her next meal would come from, only that she'd heard about an elderly woman named Shattie. So that is where she went.

Arriving at a nondescript apartment, she knocked on the front door. Shattie—a kind, wrinkled woman who'd seen many years—let her in. It was in that humble abode that she found shelter and encouragement and a good piece of calf liver to keep iron in her blood. Many months went by as she tried not to think about the abusive man she'd left and the things he had done to her and her daughter from a prior relationship. The woman suspected she was pregnant, and a myriad of questions—none of which she had answers for—raced through her mind. All she knew was that this kind elderly woman had given her some hope.

Months passed, and the day came when the pain was unbearable. By means unknown, this woman made her way to Fordham Hospital in the South Bronx. There, amidst the cacophony and bustle of the ER waiting room, she calmly informed the nurses that she was in labor. Hours later, on a hospital bed, this woman gave birth to a daughter. This baby girl had no name. All she had was a mother faced with a decision.

This mother was dignified and did not want to live on the kindness of strangers. She tossed the options around in her head and landed on two. She thought to herself, "I can either keep this child or throw her into a garbage can." A nurse holding this child arrived and placed her on the chest of the exhausted and torn mother. Something inside the woman melted as she looked at her newborn daughter. Her eyes locked with this baby girl's, and her decision was made. *I will keep this child. I will take care of this child. My life is this child.*

This child is me. The woman is my mother. The eleven-year-old daughter is my older half-sister, Debra. The abusive man is my biological father. These are the facts that my mother shared with me regarding the players in this story—*my* story. Though I was conceived, I do not know the circumstances of my conception. I never asked. My mother never told me; a missed opportunity.

Though not a big presence in my childhood, the kind elderly woman (Shattie) became the closest thing to a grandmother for me, since my mother and her own mother were not on speaking terms. Fordham Hospital is the place where I was born. The moment of decision that my mother had—to not throw me into the garbage, but keep me—was the only part of the story that she would repeatedly tell me. My mother was not the one who named me; another missed point of connection with my mom. My name—Michelle—was given to me by my 21-year-old half-sister, Lil, my mother's daughter from *another* prior relationship.

INSIGHT

This is all the information my mother told me about the circumstances under which I was born. It did not feel fair—an abusive biological father, a mom-on-the-run living off the kindness of strangers, my mother not being the one to give me my name. When these pieces of information were shared with me in dribs and drabs, I took them at face value.

> "FOR YOU FORMED MY INWARD PARTS; YOU KNITTED ME TOGETHER IN MY MOTHER'S WOMB . . ."
>
> —DAVID, THE PSALMIST

It wasn't until I'd progressed in age and eventually become a wife and mother myself that I began to reflect upon these facts—and look at myself in the mirror.

Then I realized that there were *a lot* of things my mother never told me. I guess she had her reasons. Without hearing those reasons, though, I had many assumptions and misconceptions. I guess, in my mother's mind at the time, *I* may have been a Miss Conception.

VIEW FROM THE COUCH

I am sure that my mother had valid reasons for her silence about her personal story. Her past circumstances were trying, and her then-current life circumstances didn't leave much room for snuggly evening story time accounts of the details surrounding my birth. As a child, story time was more pragmatic: it was a time for my mom to teach me to read.

But a few wonderful moments are indelibly imprinted on my memory. These were times when my mom seemed to let down her guard and let me inside her childhood in the backhills of Jamaica. She told me stories about the famous Ananse—a smart spider who always outwitted those he encountered in every situation. My mom was very animated in her storytelling as she gave all the different voices and Jamaican Patois inflections of the various story characters. She would often stand or sit in front of me when telling such stories from her culture, so physical closeness—snuggling—was not there for me. We did not regularly connect that way.

That reality did not feel fair. Oh, how I wished that she would hold me tightly—pulling me close—and let me nestle my head in her bosom and hear her heartbeat, again and again. But that was not my mom. Why couldn't she have enough energy to snuggle with me? She never told me. I never asked.

I found myself pestering her with the ongoing question: "Do you really love me?"

She'd answer, "Yes, I really love you," to which I'd reply, "Do you really, *really* love me?"

She'd reply, "I really, *really* love you."

The back-and-forth would continue until she would say several more reallys than I would say, and then—for *that* moment—I would feel convinced of her love for me. Still, I wondered: She didn't throw me into the garbage, but did she really love *me,* the child she never named?

I struggled with the uncertainty of being loved all through my childhood, tween, teen, and young adult years. I never wanted anyone else to feel that kind of uncertainty.

So when I grew up, got married, and found out I was pregnant (with twins!), I resolved to correct the Miss Conceptions I'd experienced with my mom. For starters, I knew that I wanted our children to have a different experience with me than I had as a child with my own mom. Isn't that every mother's desire? So, I made a concerted effort, as part of our twin daughters' oral history, to recount to them what was going on around the time they were born and how and why they were given their names, with all the (age-appropriate) accompanying details as they grew older. My hope was, and still is, that they would know that they were and still are loved. I love them—*who they are*—now and always.

I had many snuggly story times with my daughters when they were young. They have never once asked me *if* I love them, let alone if I *really* loved them. Come to think of it, though, when they were little, I don't recall them ever spontaneously saying "I love you, Mommy" either. That does not *feel* fair. Where did I go wrong?

It seems there is this need that I have to not *be* wrong—not *do* wrong, especially to those I love and, in particular, my daughters. But even my good intentions don't prevent me from doing the very thing I seek to avoid doing.

When my younger daughter, Jasmine, was in elementary school, she would often come into our bedroom each morning when she woke up, snuggle next to me, and tell me whatever was on her mind and heart. I loved her visits and looked forward to hearing her pour out from her heart what was occurring in her world. I would just sit and listen.

As she progressed in school and her work became more involved, I (unaware of my pattern) found that I would use that snuggly time to give Jasmine my input—unsolicited advice—on whatever she would share. Soon the snuggly time became tension time. I did not learn my lesson as the length of time Jasmine spent with me became shorter and shorter.

Eventually, the occurrence of Jasmine's visits became sporadic, with a fuss (a.k.a. an argument) ensuing each time she would walk past my bedroom door instead of coming inside to visit. Then she became "too busy" getting ready for school to visit with me. I would rationalize to myself with thoughts of, "Well, I guess she *is* prioritizing school as we've expected her to do."

But I missed our mother–daughter time together.

What did I do wrong?

What I had done wrong during our morning snuggle-time was that I'd stopped listening to her express her feelings. The snuggle-time was the time when she was learning how to face, acknowledge, manage, and express her feelings; I was her steady mirror presence giving her a safe space to see (and hear) herself as she expressed herself. However, at that time, I did not realize that this was the root of what was occurring, and I let other things take precedence in my mind's eye. That was how I lost the connection of conceiving her—hearing her and seeing her for who she was as her own person.

The result of my Miss Conception was that Jasmine no longer trusted or felt (emotionally) safe with me, the woman who'd birthed her and loved her. You might as well have taken a cleaver to my heart and cut it in two. I missed my connection with Jasmine and did not want her to experience the same disconnect I'd had with my own mother.

I needed to get back that connection with my Jasmine, and I knew I needed to change in order to regain her trust. Little did I know how long a process that would be and what kind of changes it would require from both of us.

Looking back now, I see that it's totally understandable why she began to experience me differently when I lost sight of her. What I verbally presented (*not* reflected)—my unsolicited advice—felt like criticism to her. The frequency of my unsolicited advice eroded her trust in me and clouded her vision of me as a safe place for her to open up and be vulnerable, and it clouded her vision of herself as a separate individual with valid and unique thoughts and emotions. I now see how it would've been better if, as the adult, I'd empathized with her experiences. At the time, though, I thought that just because I'd once been a tween wrestling with the angst of being a tween my speaking from that point of view would connect us. But it didn't.

It's been hard and taken a lot of effort on my part to look at myself in my mirror and the mirror of Jasmine's not-so-pretty reactions and responses to me. But it's been necessary to make changes so that she can find me to be a safe place to *relearn* how to face, acknowledge, manage, and express her feelings. This five-to-six-year process, though, has gotten us to a point where her trust in and understanding of me has been rebuilt, my connection to her has been restored, and our interest in growing our relationship has been renewed.

I don't think Jasmine has ever *enjoyed* the process, but I do hope that someday she'll think highly of me for prioritizing her, her personal growth and well-being, and our M–D Relationship.

The truth be told, though, I didn't think highly of, esteem, or prioritize developing a relationship with my mother during my early years. Granted, I knew that she worked tirelessly, but I resented her fatigue. There was not much left for me at the end of her day. That felt very unfair to me. In my mind, if I'd had an involved dad, then *he* could have borne some of the economic and emotional burden. Then life—life with me at least—might not have been such a heavy load for my mother. Maybe the young child in me worked hard to over-compensate—not do wrong—so that I would not be a heavy load, an additional burden to my mother.

VIEW FROM THE CHAIR

Experts in the field of psychology have noted that the circumstances under which a child is born will affect the mother, which in turn affect the child psychologically, emotionally, mentally, physically, and (I contend) spiritually.[2] The funhouse of life that a child will enter has mirrors that do *not* give a picture that accurately reflects

> WMNTTD
> ───────────────
> As your mom, I don't want you to experience my deepest pain.

them or their environment. Each person in that child's life has their own funhouse of mirrors that has fashioned their world. Warp begets warp. A child's mirror is warped at the time of conception.

Regarding (un)fairness, it is natural for a child to acutely feel the unfairness of life, all the while adjusting to it behaviorally. It is natural for a child to overcompensate to not feel the full pain of her lack of connection or loss of closeness with her mother.

It is natural for a mother to overcompensate—with good intentions—so that her children will not have to experience any emotional pain and so that she herself will not experience such pain again.

CRACKING THE CODE

There are pain points mothers and daughters have in their history of experiences. This carried pain fogs up their vision of themselves and each other and further clouds (warps) their mirrors. This can lead to each of them having misconceptions about themselves and others.

To crack the code of mother–daughter Miss Conceptions, you will want to observe how your personal history plays out in your interactions with your mother or daughter. You can start this observation process by asking yourself the following question:

CODE CRACKER

- What one thing about your past mother–daughter interactions do you feel was unfair?

- What are you doing now to overcompensate for it?

CHAPTER 2
FAIRNESS OF LIFE

I grew up neither expecting nor desiring to have children. I had a palpable disdain for them. As far as I was concerned, all children did was whine, cry, "suck boobies," spit up, poop, sleep . . . and then rinse and repeat. Additionally, they always made a ruckus in the most inopportune places like movie theaters, buses, planes, and restaurants. This was my conception of children . . . and of being a mother of children.

Yet, on one bright sunny spring morning in 2001, there I was—standing in a room with sky-blue, cloud-patterned wallpaper, looking out the window and holding our two-month-old twin girls in each arm. That morning, oddly enough, they were not crying.

I, however, did feel like crying. My mother-in-law, who had given me elaborate promises about being an involved grandparent, had just decided to no longer be involved in our lives. I remember the interaction as if it were yesterday.

After a strained phone conversation that had involved me listening to her criticizing my parenting ability and answering her questions, I said to her, "We would *still* like you to come over and see the girls."

She replied, "I'll let you know."

Well, she never did let me or my husband know.

On that particular spring day, as I stood holding our daughters, I unexpectedly found myself at a crossroads. As I began to realize that it would be *just* me and my BFF husband to care for our girls, a part of me started to feel overwhelmed and exhausted. Then, as I thought of my mother-in-law breaking her promise to me—which felt like a betrayal—feelings of anger began to erupt inside me. I'd expected that my daughters and I would have it better than I'd had as a child with no involved grandparents.

In that moment of decision, the stark bifurcation of my experiences and feelings jolted my senses. It was as if I'd been sucked into a DeLorean-powered time machine and taken back to the day of my birth when my mother had to decide what she would do with me—keep me or throw me in the garbage. My mom had probably felt as I did. I found myself thinking, "Did my mom feel anger toward my biological father for breaking his promise to love, honor, and cherish her?" I didn't know; my mother never told me about that. What I did know was that I could not recall her ever being truly happy—just exhausted and overwhelmed when the bills were due. Her anger came out in other ways, through her negativism and criticism when she dealt with me.

As I reflected on what I saw of myself—being overwhelmed, exhausted, and angry—in my moment of decision, I saw that my life was a far cry from my mom's life of being a single parent of two and living in an inner-city slumlord's apartment. I was happily married to a loving husband and living in a nice suburban single-family bi-level home. My expectation of motherhood—my conception in my mind's eye—was that my life would be better. In fact, on paper, my life *was* better. However, internally (mentally and emotionally), I still *felt* as if I was in the same helpless situation that my mother had been in when I was born. The whole situation with my mother-in-law didn't feel fair to me.

In my moment of decision, I could choose to keep the anger inside me and let it fester, wallow helplessly in the morass of daily maternal tasks, or become numb to it all and just go through the motions of parenting.

But then, as soon as I started to feel exhausted, overwhelmed, and infuriated, something else dawned on me. I had a fourth choice of response to my situation: *joy*.

I could choose joy. No, not the always-happy-elated-praise-God-every-moment kind of joy or the Lego-esque "everything is awesome" kind of joy you might be thinking. I mean a joyous resolve to be in-the-moment and the choice to treat every day with my daughters as special.

Why? So that I could stop our familial tendency to get weighed down by negative life circumstances. It was that moment-of-decision choice of joy that brought me back to my senses and got my will, mind, and emotions out of a potential funk that I know would've soured life, especially for my daughters. That seemed the fair thing to do for my daughters: face and deal with the difficulties before me head-on with a joyous internal resolve.

I would need that resolve because, ten months after the last phone conversation I'd had with my mother-in-law, we were served with papers suing us for grandparent visitation rights. God only knew that the lawsuit, the subsequent depletion of allocated college fund monies, and our having to take out a second mortgage on our home to pay legal fees were not and did not *feel* fair. But these circumstances occurred to me under a *fairer* set of conditions than those my mother had to face when I was born.

Life was actually being fair to me. I was not alone as my

mom had been—I was married to my BFF hubby. He and I were both gainfully employed, *and* we had awesome neighbors who had given us multiple cribs (and one who had an excellent daycare in her home—right next door to us)! I had to correct my miss-conceived expectations for what motherhood and having children might be like and reassess the internal and external resources that I'd be able to access every day.

As a mother of twin daughters, I spent those early years laser-focused on making every (well, *almost* every) moment a teachable one. I found myself looking for ways our girls could have free play, time to discover new things, books on anything and everything, and downtime to entertain themselves *without* a TV. The days *always* ended with our snuggly bedtime reading and prayer.

My goal as their mom was that by the time they entered preschool, there would not be any drawn-out separation difficulties, and there weren't. Actually, at first, I was shocked at how they readily went off into their preschool building without a second glance to see whether or not I was still standing there. I did stand there, though, and watch . . . on the first day of preschool, the first day of kindergarten, and the first day of every grade up until the bus appeared in middle school.

For the bus ride on the first day of middle school, they both kicked up a fuss because they did not want anyone to see them walking with their mother. So we compromised. I let them walk half a New York City block's distance ahead of me. That seemed fair.

VIEW FROM THE COUCH

Compromise involves *com*ing together on a *promise* to work on things together so that both parties' needs are met in a win-win kind of way. For my daughters' first middle-school bus ride, I was unseen for their vanity (daughters' win) but present enough for my sanity (my win). That seemed fair.

As my daughters have gotten older, I have heard them intimate that their teenage stage of life is unfair. Their rants have happened during times when they have not liked the set of circumstances they had to face (having to do chores the night before a test, teachers assigning them projects that are due on the same day as other subject exams, having to re-clean their bathroom because it "wasn't done properly the first time"). While, as their mom, I have yet to fully grasp what they mean by unfairness, I have surmised from their comments that fairness for a teenager means three things:

- having their personal desires/needs met (fully and immediately)

- not having to expend too much unnecessary energy to attain that desire/need

- having little resistance or no obstacles in the way of their pursuit of those desires/needs

Mmm . . . sniff sniff. Do I smell some budding sentiments of entitlement?

Entitlement is the kryptonite to developing resiliency. Resiliency is a foundation for attaining any goal in life. Resiliency allows you to bend and readjust, without breaking, as you encounter obstacles in pursuit of a goal.

Now, although the shortest distance between two points is a straight line, that line (or road) is not guaranteed to be smooth. The road to a goal is also not guaranteed to be straight; it could be circuitous or poorly lit. Realities like these can be a scary proposition for a teenage girl to acknowledge and/or navigate on her own. The unknown can be unnerving, even when someone has fairer life circumstances.

Like other well-intentioned parents, my husband and I have worked hard to provide a better—fairer—set of life circumstances for our daughters. Still, I have heard them say things and have seen reactions to situations in their lives that indicate they are experiencing the *same kinds of feelings* that I've had in my life. For me, those feelings can make things seem unfair in the moment. But then I have to remember that my current circumstances are fairer than they were for my mom, and I am able to regroup and refocus on my goal of walking in the resiliency that I saw my mom walk in time after time, day after day. Hopefully, at some point, my daughters will reach the same conclusions regarding them and me.

I regularly share with my daughters about meeting the challenges of life. But it seems that, in their own heads, they don't want to be seen with their mother (e.g. take my advice). So I have *come* to terms with the *promise* I made to them in my heart that sunny spring day in 2001. That promise was to be present and available to them with a joyous internal resolve.

I have this wish, though, that my daughters would toughen up and face hard situations directly. It makes me cringe when I see them, in their particular ways, shy away from a challenge. One part of me tries to give them the benefit of the doubt; they are just finding their way to cope with it all. Another part of me gets concerned that, if their avoidance pattern continues, they will prolong the inevitable and it might be harder for them because their internal resolve will not be strong enough.

The fact is that I cannot protect them from either eventuality. I'm not God, and even He does not always prevent adverse things from happening. But as I celebrate the birth of Immanuel (God with us) every Christmas, I am reminded that He is present with us as we go through difficulties, and in my weakness, I end up being strengthened in ways I'd not before imagined.

Adversity is a part of life that cannot be avoided. The question I ask myself, though, is how will my daughters respond to adversity? I have lived life longer than my daughters have. I can share my adversity stories, which they may or may not heed. However, I as their mom cannot drill resilience into them. My mother did not—could not—drill it into me. She *lived* resilience in front of me. But it was hard for me to watch and live alongside her in the midst of it.

VIEW FROM THE CHAIR

Resilience is a psychological construct that has been studied in the social and medical sciences. According to the American Psychological Association, resilience is defined as:

> [T]he process of adapting well in the face of adversity, trauma, tragedy, threats or significant sources of stress. . . . It means "bouncing back" from difficult experiences . . . [and] . . . involves behaviors, thoughts and actions that can be learned and developed in anyone.[3]

What makes the process of developing resiliency more difficult for daughters is that their safe place is the woman who gave birth to them. This female person—their mother—*looks like* them and has taught them what they know on some level. C.J. Boyd puts it this way:

> [M]others and daughters engage throughout their lives in *personal* identification, as opposed to positional identification. The reason for this persistence . . . is that (in Western cultures) the mother is the early caregiver and primary source of identification . . . [for] children. However, a young girl's identification with her mother continues throughout life, whereas a young boy's identification with his mother is broken and switched to his father (or another male figure). A daughter continues to identify with her caregiving mother, thereby maintaining the mother–daughter relationship while establishing her identity. A son, however, must begin to seek his identity with his . . . father, an emotional maneuver that disengages him from

the intensity of the mother–child relationship. Because of their prolonged identification with their mothers, daughters often perceive themselves as more "like" their mothers than sons are "like" their father.[4] [emphasis added]

So, a daughter's process of separating from her mom and becoming her own person is intertwined with her facing the challenges to that separation and individuation posed by her mother's mere presence and visibility within a daughter's mind. (Her internal dialogue goes something like this: "I see you, relate to you, am similar to and yet different from you. I need your instruction and guidance, but I may or may not listen to you.")

Additionally, the possibility of a daughter doing something wrong can either paralyze and prevent a daughter from taking steps to get it right or propel her to take steps to *always* get it right. Both extremes are awash with possibilities adverse to her development and M–D Relationship Dynamics (I will discuss MDRDs in Chapter 13). The mere possibility of one's mother being right from a daughter's perspective is an affront to her growing sense of her identity and independence.

WMNTTD

As your mom, I want you to overcome all adversities.

CRACKING THE CODE

A Miss Conception of motherhood is that your daughter will handle life's difficulties exactly as you did or as you think she should. Mothers and daughters need to compromise on this expectation.

The task for a daughter to develop an identity separate from her mother is tricky and requires a fair amount of balance *between* a mother and daughter and *within* each of them. A mother needs to know where her propensities intersect with her daughter's so that she can instruct, guide, and give space to her daughter as she figures out life for herself. A daughter needs to know what aspects of herself are like her mom while being okay with those similarities being expressed in ways that are different from her mother.

CODE CRACKER

- What have you compromised on with your mother or daughter?

CHAPTER 3
WHO'S THE FAIREST
ONE OF ALL?

I was sitting on our living room sofa. My twin daughters were about four months old. The youngest, Jasmine, had finally gone down for a nap, but the oldest, Candace, was not tired. So, I decided to give her some more one-on-one time and coo with her until she got tired enough to take a nap.

As I held Candace, she and I were engaged in eye-to-eye contact (an aspect of mirroring). She seemed captivated by every endearing word I spoke to her. In a familiar side-to-side rocking manner, I swayed her back and forth and finally came to a comfortable resting position with her head nestled in my forearm—which was right next to our stereo. Her head moved around as she squirmed and cooed at me. I giggled and cooed back at her.

As we engaged in this mother–daughter moment, Candace looked over in the direction of the stereo. I cooed on and smiled. Then, before I could even form the sound of her name on my lips, I saw her reach out her right hand in the direction of the big black stereo knob. Before my mind could formulate the conscious thought of *I've never told her and her sister about the stereo being off limits* and reasonably consider the situation, I immediately—but softly and lovingly—cooed, "No-no," while gently moving her hand away from the big black knob. I smiled.

Candace's face did not reciprocate my smile. I continued to gently rock her; then I paused. She was looking at the big black knob. Before I could blink, her little four-month-old hand was stretched out (again) toward the black stereo knob. With a slightly more intentional tone, I changed my countenance from smiling to flat and said with softness but more inflection in my voice, "No-no-nooo. *Don't* touch." Candace's expression became sour as I gently guided her hand back to its original position away from our stereo . . . and went back to cooing. This time, Candace was not cooing back. Instead, she had furrowed her eyebrows.

Did I just see that?

Brow furrowed. *My* baby.

Yup. I did.

My eyes blinked. Internally, I chuckled and thought to myself, "Naww. She did *not* just do that." No sooner had the word "that" crossed my mind than I saw Candace *more* intentionally put her hand out and stretch her arm until she touched the big black knob . . . *all while looking me right in the eyes!*

I thought, "Oh no she *di'n't!*"

. . . and immediately I stuck out my index finger and gave her a firm, light tap on her wrist. No, it was not a whack, just a tap that was hard enough for her to mentally and physically register some pain.

When I did this, Candace's head bopped up, and she shook her face at me with an expression of what looked like indignation. Our eyes locked.

One . . . two . . . three . . .

. . . and *then* she cried.

I knew that she *knew* my no meant no.

But I felt *so* guilty. I wondered if someone was going to call child and protective services on me for the tap. I began to replay the whole sequence of interactions in my head. I heard myself think: "I could swear this child knew *and* understood every single word I was saying and *still* chose to disobey."

I had to speak to someone. I called my husband; he said that I was not imagining things and I had responded appropriately. After I calmed myself down, I realized that he was right. (Yes, ladies, our husbands actually *do* have accurate and insightful observations!) Our daughter *did* know and understand what was being communicated to her, and she *did* act with intentional defiance. Wow! All of this wrapped up in a little four-month-old baby's body? At the time, I had no idea that this kind of awareness could exist in someone so young.

Little did I know that this dynamic of my daughter not heeding my warnings—reaching for the big black knob—and me having to redirect and instill sound counsel would play itself out many times over the years as she went through elementary, middle, and now high school.

At that moment in front of the stereo, it did not seem fair for me as her mom to have to make a choice—to tap or not to tap—during that moment of decision. In Candace's mind, the big black knob was fine to touch. For me in that moment, it was not fine for her to touch the big black knob, and it was fair to reinforce my view on the matter by disciplining Candace. Words had not worked, so I resorted to physical aversion tactics. For Candace in that same moment, the discipline was not fair and did not *feel* fair.

At each of those moments of decision, we were looking at each other. On the one hand we were connecting and checking in to see if each of us was okay with ourselves and our actions, and on the other hand, we were differentiating ourselves as not being similar in our view, intention, or experience in the matter of the big black knob. At the end of the encounter, Candace and I had a new understanding of each other that we would take into our next interaction. At the time, that seemed to be the fairest way to see things.

VIEW FROM THE COUCH

There are moments when I want my daughters to understand things from my perspective, and if they cannot do that, then at least just accept what my perspective is at face value. When they were little, they took everything I said at face value. And then, eventually, they got a mind of their own. While most of the time it is challenging for me when I feel that I have to justify what I am telling them to do or not do, it is equally fascinating to me how they take in and process the information for themselves.

The only problem is that during their teen years (often referred to by moms as the Where Did My Daughter Go? time period), daughters are doing a lot of growing and *not* much talking about the content and dynamics of how they are processing everything. To some degree, my teenage daughters still show me ways in which they've not separated from me—even as they desperately try *not* to be like me. Ugh! It'd be fairer if they gave me a chance to help them.

I guess I have to be the adult and give them a chance first to be themselves. That would be the fairest thing to do.

VIEW FROM THE CHAIR

Yale professor and psychologist Dr. Paul Bloom has been studying moral development in children and has found that infants as young as three months old can distinguish between right and wrong.[5] Still, maternal guilt about disciplining a child is a very palpable feeling. It often runs rampant in an insidious way in a mother's considerations about how to respond to her daughter's behavior. A mother's internal wrestling fluctuates throughout any given day. The trick is to find the right balance between the fairness, firmness, and frequency of every response. While the right combination of these three qualities is different for each M–D Relationship Dynamic, the most important thing to remember is that frequency is key.

By frequency, I mean the consistency of response. One is consistently either doing something or not doing something. As volitional beings, we have a dichotomy of choice. One can make a choice. One can decide *not* to make a choice, but in so doing, one *has* actually made a choice by default. Similarly, a mother can consistently apply discipline or not. The act of addressing her daughter's behavior is one thing; the act of *not* addressing her daughter's behavior is still a choice made *not* to do anything.

For a daughter, the choice is the same, but it involves choices about your degree of engagement—proactive steps to connect—with your mother. To engage or not to engage is the question; whether or not

> **WMNTTD**
>
> As your mom, it hurts when you don't give me a fair chance to get to know the real you.

it is nobler (not to be too Shakespearian about it) is not the ultimate concern.

The ultimate concern is whatever kind of result you want or desire, but it won't happen in a vacuum. Your result is determined by the choices you both decide—or don't decide— to make.

CRACKING THE CODE

I have found in my clinical work with women/young ladies/ teenage girls that mothers and daughters can spend so much time reacting rather than responding. When you react, your emotions are controlling you. When you respond, you are taking the time to understand and control your emotions. The fairest thing that mothers and daughters can do for each other is learn to slow their emotional roll and determine if what they have been doing is fair to themselves and/or the other person.

The quality of your M–D Relationship tomorrow will be the result of the decisions you make today.

CODE CRACKER

- How have you *not* been fair to your mother or daughter?

PART 2
MISS UNDERSTANDINGS
REFLECTION OR NOT

"Most quarrels amplify a misunderstanding."

—Andre Gide, *Autumn Leaves*
French Author

ASSUMPTIONS

"We got our wires crossed" is an old expression once used to explain how two people end up having a misunderstanding. The expression was an analogy based on old telecommunication systems that used an assorted labyrinth of wires, poles, and connectors to transmit the voices of people who were quite a distance away from each other. In 21st-century vernacular, an equivalent expression might be a Verizon-esque "Can you hear me now?" indicating that there is difficulty with the connection between two people.

Regardless of the expression, whenever there is difficulty or static in the relaying of information between people, those engaged in the interaction begin to make assumptions about what is being verbalized—they fill in the gaps. One benefit is that this helps move things along in the dynamics of the relationship. One potential risk, though, is that even one *incorrect* assumption may leave each person in the relationship with a different understanding—a Miss Understanding—about what has occurred between the two of them.

CHAPTER 4
DISTORTION AWAY!

It happened before I knew it. In what seemed like a mega-slo-mo clip from an *X Games* episode, I caught a glimpse of our dining room chair angling backward to the ground and—*smack!*—landing right on top of my daughter Jasmine. Her seven-month-old body was trapped under the weight of the chair.

Silence.

One . . . two . . .

I heard nothing as I got up and, as focused and steady as Wonder Woman entering a war zone, in one fluid motion extended my left arm to hoist the fiendish chair off my daughter and with my right arm scooped her off the floor.

. . . three.

Whaaaaaaaaaaaa!

The silence was broken by the piercing scream of my child.

Amidst her screams and with blood oozing from her mouth, I—with a lightning speed that downplayed the complexity of my *Matrix*-like motion around chairs and hurdling over a toy-laden floor—made my way to the kitchen. I opened the refrigerator door, extracted the magic salve and cure for all ailments—the *ice cube*—and applied it to my daughter's busted lip.

Silence. No screaming.

Calm. No commotion, just my cooing and giggling daughter in my arms. Disaster averted.

(Pan away slowly from the scene as you see me standing there victoriously with one hand on my hip and holding an ice-sucking happy child in my other arm as my Supermom cape flows effortlessly in the breeze of ease of my handling the situation!)

That is how I saw myself in that moment. Simply heroic! Very sure of myself and my ability to handle anything.

Jasmine was walking at seven months old. She was the baby who, in-utero, was always moving around and on top of her sister, Candace, who was mostly stationary. Her early mobility was not a big surprise, but I wasn't really ready for it. Back then, I had not yet figured out in my mind and heart what the ramifications would be for her to be away from my immediate physical control and supervision.

So I quickly came up with those things that would be off limits—the *no* items—in our home. With the kitchen and stairs gated off in our bi-level home, this left me with the upstairs living room and dining room which were next to each other. The only *no* items in there were the stereo with its big black knob (mentioned in Chapter 3) and the custom dining table chairs. I made sure I communicated these limitations to Jasmine on several occasions.

Jasmine was never a disobedient child; she just liked to explore. For me, both personally and professionally, exploration is foundational to learning and mastery, so I encouraged it within certain parameters. Separation from me to explore was something I believed (and still do believe) would help build a sense of independence and confidence that they would need in the short and long run. I was there whenever Jasmine and Candace returned to me with their discoveries.

Since my mother was not able to be there for me as a safe place to come back to with my discoveries and we were not relationally close, I wanted to be there for my daughters and to be relationally close (or at least closer than I had been with my mother). But first, I'd have to let them explore and be away from me.

Well, the *smack* of the toppled chair and Jasmine's three-second-delayed piercing scream brought me right back to the reality of the risks of giving my daughters such freedom.

(Pan to the right. There I am, holding a happy, ice-sucking child in my arm, but my Supermom cape has slowed its billowy roll.)

Oh my gosh! They *could* get hurt, or things could *not* go as I'd have hoped, planned, and anticipated.

My response to the toppled chairs in my daughter's life (real as well as metaphorical) has gone through many iterations over the years, and it's not always been pretty.

For example, when Jasmine was in elementary school, she would come home at the end of the school day and do her homework. She would (metaphorically speaking) separate herself from my wise parental counsel and directives to "work through the math problems step-by-step," and "practice the math homework problems more so that you can better understand them," and "it's not about the pace but the process." Despite my instruction, Jasmine did the opposite. (And yes, I acknowledge that this was disobedience, but it's homework: the last great frontier of life lessons.)

I would find myself exasperated with the situation and fume, "This child has a former math teacher for a mother, and she's not taking in or applying my input." I would then *insist* on her working through the math problems. She would resist. My insistence would increasingly become accompanied by an intense volume of words—and we would be in a World War III mode that would usually end with my fist banging the table and saying, "*Fine!* It's on you."

Now, I am not proud of those outbursts; I hate admitting them despite my having apologized to Jasmine for each and every one over the years.

I mention those outbursts to make a point. That point is that they came from a distorted (inaccurate) view that I had of my daughter. My distorted view/train of thought went like this:

- I was very good at math, and I know what the process of math mastery looks like. (True facts)

- You are a girl who is good at math but not a fan of the process. (True facts)

- You are in a school system that—according to statistics—does not support girls excelling in math, which contributes to seventh- and eighth-grade girls losing interest in math and the sciences. (True facts)

- You will *not* be a statistic. (Fear-based hope)

- You *will* master math. (Fear-based viewpoint)

- What? You're not following the first step in *my* parental process? (Flat-out fear)

- Oh no! What life and career options are you going to miss? (Fear-based projection)

- I rant. (Fear, fear, fear)

- I explode, etc. (You get the picture? This is a *far* cry from the original true facts)

Meanwhile, all Jasmine has thought and/or registered (heard) from me is:

- This math problem is hard. (Possible true fact)

- I am not easily getting the right answer. (Impatience-based fear)

- Mom is mad at me. (Experience- and fear-based true fact)

- I *should* be easily getting the right answer (Fear-based unconscious comparison: My mother easily gets the right answers; she was a math teacher.)

- Since I'm not easily getting the right answer, I am not good at math. (Fear-based conclusion)

- I don't like math since I'm not good at it. (Fear-based overgeneralization. You see where this has gone?)

So, from my one distorted view—because I was good at math, Jasmine would be like me and approach math as I had when I was her age—a whole slew of distortions has run amuck and resulted in an equation in Jasmine's mind where she sees herself as less than capable of doing math, let alone doing it well.

This fear-based view did not help her at all when she got to seventh grade and her math teacher insinuated and communicated that Jasmine was incapable. (Argh! The belephant—mama bear and mama elephant—in me started to erupt.) By then, though, I was playing catch-up and had very little ground to stand on with Jasmine as a mother who was trying to build up her daughter's self-esteem about her math abilities.

As I write this, tomorrow is the day that Jasmine will be taking the *SAT* exam for the first time. Yesterday, as I saw that she seemed stressed and on the verge of tears, I asked her what was bothering her. I simply made an observational inquiry:

"I was just wondering how you're doing and feeling because when I look at your face, you seem to be on the verge of tears."

She replied, "I'm just tired mom."

I matter-of-factly-asked, "Are you feeling overwhelmed?"

She replied, "That's an understatement."

I knew I had an in-road to ask further.

"What's making you feel overwhelmed?" I asked.

Jasmine replied, "I have to get a good score so I can get into a good college . . ." and, in tears, she worriedly snot-sobbed the rest of her feelings.

I then asked, "What kind of good score?"

She said, "I have to get a 26."

SAT scores range from 0 to 1600. My poor baby was already thinking about the ACT exam, with scores ranging from 1 to 36. She hadn't even registered for that exam yet, and she was already anxious about her results. My heart sank even more at the thought that my daughter had equated her sense of self-worth and self-confidence to a *number*. So I asked, "You think that Daddy and I want you to get a 26?" She sheepishly nodded her head. My heart ached for my daughter but then became hopeful because in her response I heard something that I could help her undo.

I said, "Booboo (my nickname for her), neither Daddy nor I have ever told you we expect a certain score. What we've said is that we expect you to try—to try to do your best. You've been studying all summer and been working on the things you don't understand, right?"

She nodded her head.

"How much of the material do you understand?"

She replied, "50%."

I said, "Okay, that's 50% more than nothing. Go and just do your best with what you have. We still and will always love you. We are in your corner and support you."

She appeared to take that in and ponder it.

I do not know if Jasmine has ever been able to forgive me for all my outbursts about the "math thing," despite my apologies to her over the years. It pains me to think about it and write about it, but I am. However well-intentioned I was or thought I was being, I was in the wrong. Period. As a result, I have done three things:

- worked on myself to get at the root of and address my maternal fears

- taken steps to find ways that will speak support and affirmation to Jasmine

- become more intentional on an emotional level with her (more about that in Chapter 14)

I've learned these approaches from my clinical clients—the brave young adult women I've seen over the years—taking note of what works to undo past hurtful dynamics and build up new, healthy interpersonal dynamics with a parent. (More about that in Section Two: The Remedy.)

It is a process, and it is doable.

VIEW FROM THE COUCH

If I had my druthers, there would be no such things as distortions. I personally don't like admitting that I—along with the rest of humanity—have them. The presence of distortions is a reminder that I have been affected by past and current experiences that have fogged the mirror of my life.

I don't like walking around in a fog. I keep knocking into things because those past (mostly negative) experiences cloud my view of those in front of me. Like those times when my older half-sister, Debra, in true Cinderella-stepsister fashion, would hurl derogatory comments at me and tell me I was stupid.

My mom attempted to counteract this by giving me pep-talks and telling me that I was not stupid but smart. Though it was hard for me to believe my mom, some of her words must have sunk in and propelled me not to be a statistic for young, inner-city Black girls. Now here I am, not a negative statistic but a small positive statistic of a Black woman in the USA who has earned a doctoral degree.

> ### WMNTTD
> ---
> As your mom, I have a fear that I won't be able to help you in the way that you need.

Although Jasmine's circumstances are quite different than mine as a young girl, I'm telling her what my mom told me: she's *not* stupid—she's smart. But I've taken it one step further and added what I never got as a child: positive affirmations and comments about her character and overall beauty. I wonder what will take root? Intelligence, character, and beauty—I pray they will all take root and blossom.

VIEW FROM THE CHAIR

Schema is a term first coined by psychologist Jean Piaget to describe the "building blocks of knowledge." In the fields of psychology and the cognitive sciences, it describes a person's "organized pattern of thought or behavior that places things into categories of information" that are used to provide a person with a framework for future understanding.[6]

A schema is usually based on some fact that a person relates to in ways that establish meaning for them. To make sense of the world around us and connect with it in meaningful and fulfilling ways, we all take in information. Then we relate to that information based on our past experiences. Sometimes, the past experiences we've had have left us feeling negatively about ourselves; this can sometimes cause us to unconsciously deny those negative feelings and instead attribute them to other people or situations—a process called projection.

Our projections onto other people or situations have some origin in truth. However, because projections can occur unconsciously (outside of our conscious awareness) and quickly, they can sometimes lead a person to make assumptions about people or situations without taking in any new information. Projections can then end up contributing to Miss Conceptions and Miss Understandings. The key to addressing this dynamic is to undergo a process of reflection to help ourselves become more *consciously* aware of our unconscious tendencies.

This is not to say that projections are a bad thing. Most of a human's unconscious material resides in the lower portions of our brainstem. This is where our earliest memories and our subsequent fight, flight, and freeze responses are housed.[7] We as humans need to learn from past experiences and rely on such information to survive and thrive in life.

For example, if you see a rose bush for the first time, reach out with your hand to pick one, and are stuck by the thorns—ouch! The next time you encounter another bush of flowers, you will unconsciously be projecting your first encounter with a bush—making assumptions based on your past experience—onto this new bush of flowers. Your body will be tentative and cautious (and with good reason) as you reach for the flower, which you may or may not pick up with your hand. Your projection of your past schema of experience has provided you with *some* (not all) information about the new bush. It's a good thing that the bush does not have feelings or unique thoughts and behaviors that are different from yours. Otherwise, you might be in for some prickly and painful Misses.

CRACKING THE CODE

If there are past outbursts or wrongs that you have done to your mother or daughter, the best (and most difficult) place to start cracking the code in the dynamics of your relationship is to apologize for the *specifics* of your contribution and ask for her forgiveness. Whether or not she forgives you is not important at this juncture; that is something she will have to decide to address within herself.

After you have apologized to her, it will be necessary for you to forgive *yourself*. This is also a process that can be difficult depending on what the issue is.

Lastly, it'll be important to take the time and the steps necessary to make *corrections* so that you minimize the likelihood of a repeat offense.

Mothers have their reasons for the things they do and don't do. Daughters have their reasons too. So, rather than ask *why* she is doing what she is doing, ask her, "What is making you feel the need to do things that way?" This kind of open-ended question will elicit more information that will enrich your understanding of each other.

CODE CRACKER

- What view do you have of your mother or daughter that you think may not be accurate?

CHAPTER 5
WHUDCHISEE...

My mother only had a primary school education in Jamaica, equivalent to an eighth-grade education in the United States. Though she never sat me down and said, "You will go to college," I understood that getting an education was essential to having any opportunity for improving life as we knew it at the time. As far as my mom was concerned, *her* job was to find honest work to maintain our food, clothing, and housing, and *my* job was to go to school and get an education with the goal of becoming a (medical) doctor, lawyer, or engineer. That was the Jamaican way in my family. Education was a means to an end.

As for the *process* of getting an education, that was another matter. My mother was too busy trying to survive in the South Bronx and the Manhattan garment district to know what I was learning or how I was really doing at school. The concepts of extracurricular activities and parent-teacher conferences were not only foreign to her but impractical.

Her choices—to go to work to earn money to keep food on the table and a roof over our heads *or* to meet with a teacher and lose a day's pay—were at odds with each other, and she often chose the former. My mom did not understand that my test scores (which were always in the 95th to 98th percentile range) indicated that she had a child with a very high IQ who would have benefited from a gifted program of some sort. When I would bring home the test reports to show her, all she could say was, "That's nice." For her, those scores and class subject grades were merely payment for our hard work. That was it.

What she did not need or expect was to come to the school (and lose a day's pay) for any non-academic (behavioral) issues. After all, she was raising me in a King's English-only Black Jamaican household in White America where correctly spoken English with no hint of a Jamaican accent, proper grammar, honesty, and well-mannered behavior were the rule. This was the first impression she always wanted me to give to others so that I could have a better future than she did. "People see what they see," she often mused. Additionally, respect and decency toward elders were expected at all times, but standing up for yourself—whatever that meant—was understood.

So, in late Autumn of third grade, when I was ushered into the Catholic school principal's office and Sister Mary Katherine said she was going to call my mother to come get me, I had to use every uterine and vaginal muscle to keep myself from peeing in my pants!

I had been in a fight—standing up for myself.

The school bully, Sylvia, was a tall, stout Black girl whose uniform and hair were always disheveled and who looked like she could've been in the WWF—as a *man!* She had been picking on me ever since school started. When she looked at me, I swear my image in her eyes must have vaporized and morphed into visions of fresh meat for her to pulverize. Verbally calling me names, physically blocking my path to the bathroom, knocking my books out of my hand, using her cronies to surround me and take my possessions away from me—you name it, she did it. None of the teachers whom I'd told and who'd witnessed these things did anything—Sylvia was bigger than they were and she often lied. So I thought there was nothing I could do.

Well, until lunchtime that pivotal Thursday. *That* day, I thought that if I could reason with Sylvia, that would be a breakthrough. But if that didn't work, I would at least dish out an equivalent *pre-planned* verbal insult instead of being insulted by her and saying nothing. (Admittedly, I was not good at the verbal-fencing done on playgrounds; it made me scared and nervous.)

I was in the lunch line, and Sylvia started up with her usual verbal assaults at me. I ignored her and sat down at the end of the lunch table. She followed me and sat across from me with her cronies on both sides of me. When she called me a name, I was so scared, but I still managed to open my mouth and mumble something back about her appearance.

She stopped chewing. She dared me to repeat my comment, and when I did, she hurled some of her food at me. Instinctively, I hurled my food back at her. Before I could blink, she had lunged across the lunch table and grabbed me *and* my hair. I grabbed her short kinky hair and began swinging to defend myself, hoping that one of my fists would land a punch so that I could get her off me. After what seemed like an eternity, some teachers split us up. They dragged her off upstairs and sent me to the principal's office.

After waiting the whole rest of the afternoon in the principal's office waiting room—knowing my mom had to ride on *two* NYC trains for at least two hours and then walk *five*

NYC blocks to get to my elementary school *and* lose half a day's pay—the door finally opened. I was not elated that my mom had arrived.

Her face was stern. Her eyes looked tired, but her body looked prepared; for what, I had no idea. She looked at me sitting in the office waiting room and said, "What happened?" I replied, "During lunch, Sylvia called me a name, I called her a name. Then she threw food at me, and I threw food back. Then she attacked me. I fought back. My teacher told me to go the principal's office. So, I've been sitting here." I could see that a match had lit a dynamite fuse as my mom's eyes narrowed and her face became like flint.

Turning her gaze from me, my mother looked at the principal's door and straightened her coat, smiling just as Sister Mary Katherine opened her office door. They shook hands with all the pleasantries as my mom was ushered into the office.

I heard the mumbled sounds of Sister Mary Katherine's voice but nothing from my mother. Then, after what seemed like forever, the office door opened. As my mother exited, she stopped right in the middle of the doorway, faced Sister Mary Katherine and said, "My daughter is a straight-A student who has been dealing with Sylvia on her own and has caused no trouble. Don't you *ever* have her sitting in an office instead of a classroom ever again. I send her here to learn; that's *your* job. I am her mother, and I discipline her; that is *my* job." Then she turned around, glanced at me (which was my cue to get up and follow her), and we both exited the building. We walked the five NYC blocks back to our apartment in silence.

So my mother *did* see me—that I was a straight-A student—and *that* meant something to her.

The next day, my mother enrolled me in a karate class.

I would not cause her to lose out on a day's pay ever again.

VIEW FROM THE COUCH

I felt violated on so many levels that Thursday: from the bullying incident to having my hair pulled in a fight to being sent to the principal's office. I was attending a predominantly Irish-Italian parochial school in the South Bronx. My mom worked two jobs to pay the tuition. I was not the only Black student at the school, but I was *the* top performing student who also happened to be Black. What was mind-boggling to me at the time was how quickly my King's English upbringing and well-behaved, straight-A-student reputation was flung aside by a White school administrator. Whudchisee? The administrator had been quick to see, categorize, and treat me as a ghetto ruffian, which I was not. I did not know what to think as I waited in the principal's office.

That is, until my mother exited Sister Mary Katherine's office. Whud-eye-see? I saw my mom's countenance of confident resolve. Then I heard her say, "Don't you ever have her sitting in an office instead of a

WMNTTD
As your mom, I believe the best about you and need to trust you so that I can have your back.

classroom . . . I am her mother, and I discipline her; that is *my* job." I felt vindicated. First, because my mom believed me. Second, she defended me by taking a stand on what someone could and could not do to me. Third, she verbalized everything in public (in front of me and the principal). She was my hero that day—my Trojan.

My bond with my mom was predicated on trust and the understanding that we each knew our roles and the goals toward which we were working. What I saw that day was our dynamic, our bond, working synchronously.

VIEW FROM THE CHAIR

Racism is when the systems of a dominant race and its members are established by and result in a race-based advantage that is pervasive over a minority racial group and its members.[8] One would be sorely remiss to overlook and/or ignore the experiences of minority children within a public or private school system. One would be equally short-sighted to downplay or negate the impact of such racial realities on parents who may be "doing the best they can with what they've got." I think the American playwright Eve Ensler said it best:

> "... the greatest illusion we have is that denial protects us. It's actually the biggest distortion and lie ..."[9]

It is incumbent upon administrators and complementary social support services personnel to make an effort to get to know their racial minority students personally so that those students and families within their purview will thrive. Racism does not see; it is quick to assume. It is necessary to help parents navigate systems that are quick to make assumptions about and not *see* their child.

It is important for parents to establish appropriate boundaries with their children and school personnel early on regarding their parenting role. They also need to follow through and work collaboratively with teachers and administrators regarding academic and disciplinary matters. Respect is a two-way street.

Daughters can help their cause by establishing and maintaining honest and open communication with their mothers so that they can appropriately advocate for (or coach them to advocate for) their needs and interests.

CRACKING THE CODE

Take a week to observe your mom or daughter. Write down any positive or helpful deeds she's done toward/for you or another person. Tally them. Then take another week to find ways to express gratitude to her for each of those specific or similar instances.

CODE CRACKER

- What is a positive quality/manner/essence that you see in your mother or daughter?

CHAPTER 6
...IZWHUDCHAGET

My mom and I had a kind of Penn-and-Teller dynamic in our bond. She had a Penn-ish panache and flair in her presentation of herself (and me, by extension). Back in her home country of Jamaica, despite having only an eighth-grade education, her acumen for creative fashion design and her seamstress skills had garnered a noticeable reputation for her within her local island community. She never spoke much of that time in her life or what prompted her to leave my eldest half-sister, Lil, with relatives in Jamaica and take my next eldest half-sister, Debra, with her to America. All she would say to me—in the broken Patois dialect that she never spoke in public—was, "Me was a well-known seamstress boc' un d' islan'."

The fact that my mom could think of a design and—without using any precut sewing design patterns or tape measure—take any material and whip it into a tailored outfit

51

was nothing short of magic. Well, that is what I think about her talent now. During my early childhood, however, I did not think much of it. Her seamstress skills simply saved us money.

For example, when the local Catholic schools I attended required the purchase of uniforms, my mother simply looked at the samples that were brought into the school and then wrinkled up her nose with contempt at "d' poor craftsmanship" (as she put it). Then she'd go out to several fabric stores to find the best price for the materials. In less than a week, after pulling double shifts in the sweatshops and then a third shift at home hunched over her secondhand Singer sewing machine in the middle of the night, she would have at least two sets of uniforms made and ready for me to wear.

She received no accolades from anyone—only my unappreciative eye rolls (performed with a Teller-esque slumped body) as she spun me around to see her magic displayed. No applause—only a few dollars saved for the bills that were due last week. No designer deals from the Tim Gunns and Zach Posens of the *Project Runway* industry—only the obscurity of a mother trying to make ends meet.

It was probably this daily grind of making ends meet with no financial assistance from my biological father that fueled the frustration that ignited one day when I was four years old. She dressed me up that Sunday morning and took me on a bus and a train to a place where the streets were unfamiliar to me (I later learned those unfamiliar streets were in Brooklyn). We walked into a church building and sat through the service. When it was over and most of the people had cleared out, she pointed to a man who had been sitting on the stage during the service and told me to "go up de' an' tell 'im, 'I'm ya dawta.'"

Walking that 25-foot distance felt like I was walking the length of a football field in slow motion. The man had been talking to two other men. When I got near him, the other men had to motion to him that I was standing there before he turned to face me.

(Stop film! Mute the background noise. Switch to slow-mo footage.)

The man turned in my direction. I said what my mother told me to say.

He said nothing. He turned away and went back to conversing with the other men.

(Resume background noise and regular film speed.)

I walked back to my mother who was sitting in the pew. She looked at me, "What 'im se?"

I replied, "Nothing."

With that, my mom's face stiffened. Her chest sucked in air to propel her to stand up, take my hand, and walk out of the church building. She said nothing on the train and bus rides home. *Neither* the man nor my mother *saw* me that day. They were caught up in their own thing.

Many *other* people had seen me, though, and had told my mother that I was "a special child" and "such a cute child." So a few months after that trip to Brooklyn (after she had saved enough money from working overtime), my mom enrolled me in a modeling class where promising students were offered an opportunity to sign with a modeling agency or agent.

After weeks of "hold your head up," "lead with your hips," and balancing books on my head, I finally made the cut and signed with the Selma Rubin Talent Agency. Rubin was the agent for such talents as Ralph Carter who played Michael Evans on the TV show *Good Times*, Donny Most who played Ralph Mouth on *Happy Days*, and Academy Award winner Irene Cara who sang "What A Feeling" for the soundtrack of the movie *Flashdance*. My mother's hopes were ignited. She saw me as her money ticket, with her ROI having more potential than the future medical degree toward which I'd been making progress with my stellar grades.

Days, weeks, months, and years of interviewing ensued, followed by rejection after rejection. Finally, after two years, I got my big break with a *Sara Lee* orange-flavored cake commercial.

After that, more opportunities came. Though I didn't earn a ton of money (compared to what actors make for commercials nowadays), to a single mom raising two kids in the South Bronx and working in the sweatshops, my paychecks had more digits before the decimal point than she had ever seen.

Though my mother's efforts and labor were not seen, affirmed, or valued at home or in her workplace, I—her cute, special daughter—*was* being seen and externally affirmed and valued with money; money that she saw herself banking on later. My mother saw herself as having nothing of any material value and no viable financial stability or future for herself as she got older. I was no longer just her daughter: I was her way out of poverty.

That is what my mom had thought until I graduated from Brown University and decided to move from the South Bronx to Tarrytown, NY, to take a teaching job at a private school. That was the day when I informed her that I would be withdrawing my money from the bank to start my adult life. That was the day I heard for the first time words that ripped my heart in two.

"How could you! Dat money was to stay 'ere. I thought you would gimme dat money."

"No, mom. It's my money. I need it now to get my life started."

Then the knife-sharp reply: "Me disappointed in you." She went further, "You not de daughter me raised."

I looked at her in silence. I could not believe what I had just heard.

Then she said with a huff, "Fine. Den if you go like dat (with your money), you dun't have a place to kum boc to."

I'd thought—assumed—that through all those years of toil, our bond was in sync and solid. I'd thought—again, *assumed*—that we had an understanding: she'd work at work, and I'd work at school, get a great education, and then make a life for myself. Those first two items are what I saw, and that's what I got. The last item—making a life for myself—I was still pursuing. I thought I'd had a pretty good track record of success that deserved some acknowledgement. However, instead of getting a supportive "I'm glad to see you being so responsible and wise with your life and decisions," what I got instead was the rug of (false) reality pulled out from under me. My new reality was that my mom's support had been based on my attaining some kind of socioeconomic status and giving her financial payback for the time and effort she'd put into raising me.

What I saw more clearly on that day is what I got, and it hurt deeply. Especially the D word. That experience impacted the way I approached my life from that point onward. I felt and believed that I had to get things right because I had nothing—no one—for a safety net.

Do you hear any fear in there?

When I became a mother, I resolved *never* to use the word *disappointed*. However, I *have* used the M word (money) a lot. As soon as our girls grasped the concepts of addition and subtraction, which was quite early, I introduced the concept of money to them. They heard me say that money "makes the world go 'round," something that is *earned* as a result of honest hard work—it is not spat out of an ATM from nowhere.

For example, when my daughters got paid for doing simple jobs around the house (making their starter beds at 18 months old or sweeping the kitchen floor at five years old), I applauded and showed them how to spend their earnings. First, give their 10% to God as a form of thanks for His helping them have the strength and ability to do their jobs; second, save half of the remainder for the long-term (nice big treats later); and third, keep the remaining half to spend responsibly.

There would be times when I was out shopping with them and they'd insist that I buy a particular treat for which I'd not budgeted or a school supply "with the doggy" picture that was not on sale. In these instances, I would quip, "You could use *your* money to buy that; you have enough." Though it wasn't my intention, that comment would always stop their fussing.

I remember one day when our girls came home from first grade. They were attending a private prep school at the time. In their account to me of their day, they both mentioned how the teacher had said that they needed to bring in certain supplies to do a class project. Realizing that they did not have enough money in their spending stash, the girls told their teacher, "Our mother makes us buy our own school supplies, and right now we don't have enough money." Needless to say, when I heard this I busted out laughing.

On the inside, though, I felt embarrassed by their innocent yet accurate communication to their prep school teacher and privileged classmates about how our family did money. I didn't want anyone to think that we couldn't afford to pay for something as simple as school supplies.

On the other hand, I was mystified by the way our girls had internalized my comments, which were meant to make them aware of the value of a dollar. What they had seen and experienced in *their* reality—"My parents expect me to pay for things using money I earned"—was the result of *my* reality. I experienced the effects of having another person tie their monetary hopes to my neck as well as the benefits of earning my own money and deciding how to spend it.

I wanted a different—better—experience for my daughters.

But since we had to use all the money that had taken years to save for our daughters' college expenses to fend off their paternal grandparents' lawsuit for visitation rights, our girls do not have the kind of cushion that I had hoped would make things easier for them. Instead, they are faced with the same kind of financial realities that I had to face when I was their age: not having any personal financial resources to foot the bill for college. In all honesty, though, I never expected to be able to pay for all of their college tuitions. I just never wanted them to have to experience *any* net being pulled out from under them.

VIEW FROM THE COUCH

My mother and I had an "understanding." The problem was that much of this understanding was unspoken. Unspoken understandings are laden with assumptions which breed misunderstandings.

> "ASSUMPTIONS . . . BREED MISUNDERSTANDINGS. UNADDRESSED MISUNDERSTANDINGS LEAD TO RIFTS."

Unaddressed misunderstandings lead to rifts (insurmountable fights, tiffs, and separations) that stress an M–D Relationship.

Would I rather have my daughters stressed about financial concerns instead of stressing about conflicts with me, their mom? Yes. But in all honesty, I would prefer that they not be stressed at all. I know that kind of expectation is not realistic, though. We all need *some* stress in our lives. It keeps us on our toes, right?

I was just hoping that I could mitigate their stress a tad bit by making them aware of the source of money—that I was not the source of their money as my mom had seen me. I want my daughters to see that they have the requisite skills, talents, and disciplined work ethic within themselves to put forth consistent work and effort to earn and acquire the resources that they need. I would have preferred to teach them this with a financial cushion, though.

I also want them to know that they don't have to worry about being financially responsible for me (or my husband) in any way. I don't ever want to saddle them with that kind of burden, whatever my financial state may be when I am old. (Mmm. Could there be any fear-based projections in *that* statement?)

VIEW FROM THE CHAIR

A 2015 Pew Research Center report found that 66% of caregivers for aging parents are female. Of those adults with parents aged 75 or older, 58% say that they've helped parents with errands, housework, and home repairs, 28% say they've helped financially, and 14% say they've provided personal care. 88% find this responsibility to be rewarding while 32% admit that it's a struggle.[10]

> **WMNTTD**
>
> As your mom, there are things that I feel and/or believe about myself that I am afraid to share with you (e.g. that I need you).

It is clear that caring for aging parents is a life transition that can be mentally, emotionally, and financially stressful for all involved, and it is particularly stressful on M–D Relationship bonds.

So it is completely normal for a mother not to want to switch roles with her daughter acting as the caretaker, especially if their M–D Relationship is already strained. Some other reasons that may contribute to a mother clinging to her independence are

- loss of control
- fear of rejection and/or abandonment
- guilt and shame

Unresolved Miss Conceptions and Miss Understandings scratch up the glass mirror in which a mother and daughter see themselves and each other. What they each see will impact what they get. Additionally, how they interact with what they see will affect how they navigate transitions like developmental role switches.

CRACKING THE CODE

A mother of a teen daughter would do well to ask her what she may be dreading about any upcoming life transitions. If she's already in the midst of a life transition, ask her how she is feeling about it all.

A mother and daughter who are older would do well to have The Conversation about what they are thinking, fearing, and/or feeling about aspects of the anticipated life transitions they will each face. Additionally, having a heart-to-heart talk about finances may be difficult, but it is important. You don't want any financial surprises popping up at a bad time. The key is to realize that your messages about money have shaped your current views of money and each other.

CODE CRACKER

- What assumptions do you think your mother or daughter has about you?

PART 3
MISS COMMUNICATIONS
CRACKED LENSES

"Miscommunication leads to complication."

—Lauryn Hill, from the song "Lost Ones"
Singer/Songwriter

BUSTED

In the age of technology and the internet, the notion of communication has expanded to include not only the giver and recipient but also the various mediums used to transmit information. At its core, though, communication between two people requires that the giver and recipient be

- present and available

- open and receptive

- forthcoming with information

When a telephone pole breaks and the wires come tumbling down, cables get cut, or there is interference in the cable signal, then one could say that the lines of communication just got busted. Similarly, with communication between two people, any number of factors can contribute to communication lines getting busted.

Mothers and daughters are notorious for assuming that their woman's intuition will help them communicate telepathically so that the other will "just get it" about them and what is going on in their lives.

The next three chapters will address ways in which busted protections, expectations, and relationships can interfere with a mother or daughter being present and available, open and receptive, and forthcoming with information.

CHAPTER 7
BUSTED PROTECTIONS

He could do no wrong. A tall, slender, bearded West Indian engineer named Jerome had married my eldest half-sister, Lil, who was a nurse. In the Jamaican world, she had hit the social jackpot. My mother never told me how Lil and Jerome had met; I never heard any stories of dating or courtship. Simply put: when I was born, he was there.

Lil and Jerome lived in an apartment in another section of NYC; I was not told specifically where. Whenever they would visit my mom and me at our South Bronx apartment, there was great anticipation of their arrival. My mother, a magician in the kitchen, would whip up something from the bare cupboard, and soon the aroma of home-cooked Jamaican cuisine would fill the rooms. Everything revolved around what would make Jerome comfortable because he worked so hard at his engineering job.

Things got really exciting when Lil and Jerome were able to move into their first single-family home with a white picket fence. Then, four years after I was born, my niece Charlotte arrived as their newborn bundle of joy. Charlotte and I were the babies in the family, and everyone expected the two of us to hang out and play together. My mother began sending me over to Lil's house to play. However, it seemed to me that my mom was more interested in my staying in an *actual home* than in my having the opportunity to have a playdate with someone my age. So, on any given Saturday, Lil and Jerome would pick me up in their Chrysler and drive me over to their house for the day.

One time when I was about five years old, I heard Mom talking to Lil about me staying over at their house for the weekend. I was excited! I'd get to spend a whole weekend with my big sister!

I got picked up on a Friday evening. At their house, I hung out wherever Lil was and occasionally played with Charlotte. Then it was time to get ready for bed. I heard Lil tell Jerome to make sure the kids got a bath.

I got my toothbrush and pajamas ready. Lil gave me a washcloth and towel, and I made my way to the bathroom. As I was brushing my teeth in the bathroom, Jerome came in, turned on the faucet to the bathtub, and left. I got my clothes off and, washcloth in hand, got into the tub and sat down. The water was up to my hips. I got the bar of soap and began to lather up my washcloth.

The bathroom door opened. I was startled. It was Jerome. He was holding a butt-naked Charlotte in his arms. He put her in the tub with me, poured a cap of bubble bath, and began bathing Charlotte. Having lived in a not-so-nice apartment in the South Bronx that had peeling walls in the bathroom, a rusty-piped shower, and a dingy-colored bathtub, bubble baths were not something I regularly had. So I got wrapped up in the bubbles, the splash of the water (from Charlotte), and the feel of a pristine, smooth-surfaced bathtub. It was a treat. It all felt great. Until . . .

I feel the terrycloth-covered hand of a man rubbing the outside of my vagina. Wait. I was washing my own body; I'm old enough to do that.

Then there's the rubbing of his fingers on my "thing."

That feels different. What is that?

He's looking at me and looking at the bathroom door. Now he's looking at Charlotte.

Wait! What's that?

His fingers are prying into my "hole." That does not feel good.

I do not say anything. I just look at him.

I'm confused. I do not feel right.

He looks at the door, takes Charlotte in his arms, gets up, and says something to Lil.

Then he's gone.

I'm left there in the bathtub, alone.

"Mommy!" I want to call out. Wait, my mom's not with me.

"Lil?" I want to cry out, but nothing comes out of my mouth. My voice feels stifled.

I slowly get out of the tub.

I cannot dry all of myself with my towel. I cannot touch my private area.

I feel wrong.

I get into my pajamas.

"Lil . . ." Her name forms on my lips in a hushed whisper.

"Lil." Her name sounds louder in my head.

"I'll go tell Lil," I think to myself.

By the time I gathered up my belongings, turned off the bathroom lights, and opened the door, the hallway lights were off. The only light was a flickering blue-grey hue coming from the living room down the hall. I walked slowly toward it and peeked around the entryway.

There on the couch were Lil and Jerome cuddled up together watching TV.

My heart sank.

My foot must have accidentally knocked something because Lil looked up in my direction and, smiling, she asked, "You want to come join us?" In a microsecond, I glanced at Jerome, who seemed not to register my presence, and sheepishly replied, "N-no, thank you."

I turned around and went to my assigned room and fell asleep.

The next day, I kept trying to find the right time to talk to Lil. But the "right time" never came. *He* was always there.

When bath time came, I convinced myself that I'd just imagined the prior night's bath time *thing*.

> *"This is Jerome after all," I think to myself. "It must be okay."*
> *Wait.*
> *I just told him that I can bathe myself, yet he just took the washcloth from me and is cleaning me . . .*
> *. . . why's he telling me to spread my legs.*
> *Hey, wait!*
> *He's getting rough. His finger is rough.*
> *Ouch!*
> *He's just staring at me.*
> *Why can't I scream? No words are coming out of my mouth.*
> *He's done. He's gone.*
> *I want to go home.*

Sunday could not arrive quickly enough. Lil and Jerome dropped me off back at our apartment. Mom was there. She was all smiles, as were Lil *and* Jerome.

I had no expression on my face. No one noticed.

It'd be my word against his. Jerome can do no wrong.

My mother would not believe me if I told her what happened.

I can't say anything.

I didn't say anything.

Weekend visits became a normal part of our family's routine for the next four to five years. Mom would get a break from taking care of me. I would get a "better experience" being in a white picket-fenced house with my eldest half-sister and her "perfect, can-do-no-wrong" husband.

However, the "better experience" became a routine bitter experience for me as the fondling, probing penetration and rough rubbing on areas of my body—molestation—evoked sexual sensations and physical pain that I'd never before experienced. With each regular encounter with Jerome, I found myself sinking into a silence that eroded my conscious sensibilities like cancer. That silence left me acquiescing to a normalized abnormality and succumbing to erotic and guilt-inducing masturbatory practices.

So when Lil and Jerome's second baby bundle, Derek, arrived four years after Charlotte, and Jerome (still in charge of bedtime bath time) corralled *all* of us into the bathtub, I did not register it as strange. I *did* register that I was in a bathtub with a boy with his exposed "thing" dangling there in front of me.

I also registered that I—*not* Charlotte—was the one Jerome told to "spread your legs."

Maybe that was one of the core reasons why Charlotte and I were never really close. I don't know. My mind and emotions are wandering now even as I write this.

I definitely know that my mind began to wander after our twin daughters were born.

Despite our having no involved grandparents helping us out, my BFF hubby and I rocked it! We work well together as a team. To use a basketball analogy, if he sees that the ball is not moving down the court, he will pick it up and do whatever is needed to help the team make progress and score a basket. When he saw that after his two-week paternity leave from work I would be caring for our girls all day with no help, he took it upon himself to do *all* the nighttime feedings so that I could get sleep.

We each pitched in to do whatever needed to be done; while reading parenting books like *Touchpoints* by Dr. T. Berry Brazelton,[11] taking parenting classes at the local hospital, and giving each other encouragement to help ourselves along.

However, as the girls were about to get to the point of being able to sit up in a bathtub, I began to "feel some kinda way" (as they say here in the South) about the bathtub thing. What I did *not* anticipate were the jittery, palm-sweating, gut-clenching fears about baths being given by anyone except me. My BFF hubby already knew about Jerome, totally understood, and was not offended in the least when I asked that I do all the bathing of our daughters until they were old enough to do it on their own.

And I made sure that I (in a hands-off way) taught both of them how to bathe themselves *by* themselves.

VIEW FROM THE COUCH

I don't like thinking about Jerome. As I grew older, I began to distance myself from him—emotionally and physically—and kept things professional. I never wanted him to walk me down the aisle or have the father-daughter dance with him on my wedding day. That was something that my mother assumed, talked about, and expected would happen for her baby girl who'd grown up without her biological father. Jerome was the man of the house—the male presence in our family. He

70

was the person who stayed married to Lil and made a decent living as an engineer.

This is how my mom saw things, and she assumed I saw things the way she did. We never talked about it. We missed communicating about it and Miss Communicated about our M–D Relationship.

Tears well up in my eyes as I look back and think about the bath time "routine" with Jerome and how *this* was the person whom everyone in my family expected to walk me down the aisle and represent fatherhood to me. My eyes are watery as I think about how much more pain it would have caused my mother if I had told her my *real* reasons for not wanting Jerome to "have the honor" of giving me away at my wedding. (There he was again—*his presence*—silencing my voice.) At the time, there was no one in my life—other than God the Father—who represented *real* fatherhood to me.

That is until I married my BFF.

Though I do realize that no one on this side of life's curtain is perfect, I can say that my BFF hubby stands head-and-shoulders above the rest. His kind and gentle way with our girls reveals a man who has an understanding of the importance of laying down his life daily, leading with a servant's heart, clearly delineating appropriate boundaries and exemplifying respect for personal space, speaking the truth in love, and giving wise counsel—just to name a few of his awesome qualities (which he'd never say about himself).

For me to have been and continue to be a recipient of such qualities as his wife and then to see him daily live out those same qualities with our daughters brings tears to my eyes every time. I don't deserve him, but I'm glad I have him, and I am glad that he is the father of my daughters.

Looking back now, 25 years

WMNTTD
As your mom, there are things in life that I myself am still trying to make sense of.

after my wedding day, I wish I could've told my mother about Jerome back then when things were happening in real-time. It would've been a difficult thing for her to hear. Why? Because in her mind Jerome could do no wrong. Thinking about it now, I don't think that back then I had the requisite tools or understanding to engage in such a conversation. By not having those tools, I missed out on an opportunity to communicate with my mom about my busted boundaries and the effect they had on me.

VIEW FROM THE CHAIR

Over the past 20-plus years of work with clients who've experienced trauma and abuse, I have helped women (and men) not only find the courage to face their pain but also find their voice to express themselves in a way that facilitates healing in their lives.

Though the overall process is hard, for the majority of my clients it is the finding of their voice to express themselves that poses the greatest challenge. Finding their voice involves two difficult steps:

1. verbalizing the pain to others complicit in the trauma

2. verbalizing the pain to the entity/person who inflicted the trauma (although this is not always possible)

During the process of verbalizing their pain to others— especially those who knowingly or unknowingly were complicit in the trauma—the person has to face the possibility of

- not being believed

- being called crazy

- being ostracized/shunned (again), thus re-experiencing their past pain in the present day

If they are not guided through this process by a steady, supportive, safe, validating person (e.g., a trauma-trained state-licensed mental health clinician), the likelihood of the person digressing into non-optimal life patterns increases. During the process of verbalizing the pain to the perpetrator of the trauma, the traumatized person has to be clear about four things:

1. their separate, self-sustaining identity via the establishment of appropriate (physical, mental, and emotional) boundaries

2. the degree of control they have over their responses

3. the amount of responsibility they don't have over the perpetrator's reactions

4. the possible ramifications of the confrontation and having appropriate pre-determined actions to take in order to maintain their safety

Well-meaning and/or aware mothers and daughters will normally feel remorse, guilt, and shame if they were complicit, unavailable, or unable to stop past traumatic events from happening. These are normal and natural feelings, and they need to be processed.

CRACKING THE CODE

As early as possible (but especially before girls start kindergarten), mothers need to start introducing their daughters to the concepts of boundaries and personal space. I know from conducting parent workshops on such matters that there are a few items that ought to be addressed here.

Though every family and culture have different standards in the areas of boundaries and personal space, at the bare minimum, a daughter needs to be told that her "no" will be and ought to be respected by everyone. As she gets older, this will come into play socially, but the practice arena can be within the immediate and extended family.

For example, if little Jane does not want to give Uncle Steve a hug on a particular day, then you, mom, need to back up your daughter's wishes. Or if you observe your daughter's discomfort with Aunt Sue pinching her cheeks, then (depending on Jane's age) you will need to either have a talk with Aunt Sue or coach Jane on how to appropriately voice her preference for no cheek pinching to Aunt Sue.

If you are an older daughter involved in your mother's life and you notice that she is not being treated well by someone, then talking with your mom about your observations and concerns will convey your love and help her (re)prioritize herself. If you notice that she is not being treated well at a senior living facility, you may have to advocate for her.

CODE CRACKER

- What is that thing you've not been able to say or talk about with your mom or daughter?

CHAPTER 8
BUSTED EXPECTATIONS

After physiological needs (shelter, food, sleep, etc.), safety ranks second on Maslow's hierarchy of needs that are foundational to a person's development.[12] Safety is essential to one's overall sense of well-being.

A child expects to be kept safe. They come out of the womb with an unspoken assumption that their parent(s) will keep them safe. That sense of safety informs and impacts how a child grows and navigates the world in which he or she lives.

As a child, my world was *not* safe. While living in the South Bronx had its share of external geographical hazards, most of my daily hazards were within my own immediate family. When I was young—likely not older than four or five years old—my mother told me that on the day I was born, my half-sister Debra took one look at me and commented, "Well, there goes my birthright." I'm not sure, though, what monetary inheritance she may have been expecting given the abject poverty in which we both lived. Maybe, for her, "birthright" meant my mom's full attention.

Whatever "it" was that Debra felt she was no longer getting from our mom, she was not happy about it at all. She had strong feelings about her life and, by extension, my life, and she never hesitated to physically, verbally, and emotionally take her anger out on me. This abusive pattern was mitigated a bit when I was younger because my mother would take me either to Shattie's or a babysitter's apartment. But when I started attending first grade and was able to walk home from school as a latchkey kid, things got worse. I was home alone with Debra while mom was at least a one- to two-hour train ride away at work in the Lower Manhattan garment district.

My mother knew that Debra beat me. She would often encourage me to "not pay her any mind" or "just go to your room when she gets that way." I tried to follow my mom's advice, but it never seemed to work. The beatings would just keep happening.

One day, though, after Debra had beaten me badly enough to bruise me more than usual, I showed my mom what Debra had done to my body. Her lips quivered as she bit them. Her brow furrowed, but with hesitation. She knew that Debra was in the living room. She also knew that the situation had gone too far and needed to be addressed. Mom told me to stay in the kitchen. Then she walked down the long hallway of the apartment to the living room.

At first, I heard nothing. Then, "Debra, she's your sister," came my mother's faint voice.

"She's *not* my sister! She's a brat! You had her!" bellowed Debra at a thunderous volume.

More words were exchanged even more intensely.

I slipped out of the kitchen table chair and slowly slid my back against the hallway wall, tiptoeing so as not to be heard during the silent moments.

"You're her big sister. You're supposed to look after her when I'm not here."

"You're *never* here!"

I heard a chair scratch on the living room floor, followed by another chair's sliding screech. Then footsteps thumping.

"Come on, be reasonable, Debra." My mom began to explain her reasons for having to work.

Then Debra said something referencing her own biological father, to which my mom replied pleadingly, "That's not fair!"

Debra's voice sounded like a volcanic eruption, "You always prefer that f—ing brat!"

"Watch your language when you're speaking to me!"

Before I knew it, I heard a table being pushed.

I raced to the dining room's glass-paned swinging doors to see Debra push my mother to the ground, pick up a loose bicycle stand, and whack her on the head.

Thud!

I quickly ran to my room, closed the door, and huddled in the corner near my bed. Debra's footsteps thundered to the closet, then out the front door.

SLAM!

She was gone.

I slowly made my way to the dining room to find my mother sitting on a chair with her right hand holding her bloodied head. In that moment, my expectations about my mother's ability to protect me were shattered. My *one* source of protection—my Trojan—was not as strong as I'd once thought. My mom had given me shelter, food, and a place to sleep at night—my physiological needs. But she could not keep me safe. On that day, my world became even more dangerous.

My mom's eyes were hollow with the realization that even after leaving her abusive husband, all her efforts to provide a safe home for me were for naught. She was not successful in her goal to keep her baby girl or herself safe.

Furthermore, she was a single mom, and the prospect of her experiencing a loving relationship (third item on Maslow's hierarchy) with a man was nowhere on the horizon. She had not had a great relationship track record given that her three daughters were from three different men. She was left to find other ways to bolster her self-esteem (fourth in the hierarchy).

With no white-collar career prospects for herself, my mom turned her attention to me. She turned her focus from the pain of her failures and shortcomings to the prospect (the hope) of my becoming a medical professional. For me to accomplish this professional goal would result in the respect and monetary reward that would enable me to buy a nice home with a white-picket-fenced yard for her to live out the rest of her days in safety. Additionally, she would have social recognition ("My daughter's a doctor."), which would be a balm of satisfaction for her self-esteem.

However, I do not think my mom was fully aware or convinced of how much was involved in the educational process of becoming a medical doctor. We Miss Communicated about that kind of stuff. Much of my academic performance—being a straight-A student with numerous math and science awards—throughout my K–8 school years seemed like side notes to my mom. She never made mention of them except to other Jamaicans when we had company over to the apartment or if we went out to a social gathering.

Because I appeared in TV commercials and print ads as a child, my mom had tangible evidence for social bragging rights. That did not appear to be enough for her, though. It seemed to me that she wanted to prove that I—the child *she* birthed—had talent. Every time we had a gathering at our apartment, my mom expected me to musically and vocally perform on cue for company.

I did not like those social encounters. The whole ordeal of playing the piano in front of company was a task I loathed, and I usually botched it up in some way that did not meet her expectations. The look of disappointment and embarrassment on her face became all too familiar. I hated that look.

Which was I to be? A trained seal or a trained scientist?

My mom never mentioned or bragged about any of my athletic performances or the numerous athletic awards I received, even to other Jamaicans! My athletic ability did not register as an accomplishment, so much so that one summer I had to bring her a point-by-point justification for why she should send me to a one-week basketball camp in Upstate NY (which, after saving up the money, she reluctantly did).

View from the Couch

It seemed like I expected my mom to be my ultimate protector and she was expecting me to be her ultimate provider, both expectations stemming from a natural need and desire for safety. The only difference was that my need for safety stemmed from the innate expectation of a child while my mom's desires seemed to stem from an unmet need for safety in her interpersonal relationships.

Her needs morphed into an expectation that I could not meet as a child and which fogged her view of me. My expectations dissolved into resentment and apathy about not being seen for who I was: a smart, intelligent, science- and math-oriented *and* gifted girl, student, and athlete. All in all, our communication lines were busted indeed; we had no common ground for connection.

As a mother of twin girls, it was instinctive for me—as for any well-meaning mother—to work toward providing a safe environment for my daughters. Such an instinct is never more clearly felt than when a daughter goes off to school for the first time. Anticipating the inevitability of my baby chicks leaving the nest—albeit only for several hours—I spent considerable time preparing them for their departure. In age-appropriate language and terms, I covered topics like

- personal space
- verbalizing no at school
- looking out for your sister
- acceptable and unacceptable physical contact

In the midst of their play, I'd join in and playfully run through various scenarios with them, listening to and observing their responses and interjecting strategies (wording, phrasing, demonstrations) for how to address each situation—all before they went to pre-K.

For example, if they were playing with their dolls, I would listen to the animated stories they'd tell. If a scenario occurred in their storytelling ("there she goes up the elevator . . ."), I would join in using one of their dolls ("An older person enters the elevator with her. Where are her mommy and daddy? Maybe she should go get them."). When they finished their playtime, I would engage them in an age-appropriate discussion about elevator situations: when they would be old enough to go into an elevator by themselves, how to discern a potentially unsafe situation, and ways to avoid it.

As they progressed through school, I reinforced these and similar topics in the way I interacted with them or in the way I'd intervene in any instance of a "that's miiiinnnne" whining moment. ("You need to respect her space and her toy.")

Starting in third grade, I expanded the scenarios to include boy and girl behavior patterns and mindsets. I was on top of things and happy that I was being proactive about acclimating our girls for life in a preventive way. Because our family life is predicated on love and respect, the topics I'd covered seemed sufficient.

> ### WMNTTD
> As your mom, I don't want you to get stuck in painful patterns.

My foresight had a blind spot, though, that was quickly given a black eye. In middle school, we learned that one of our daughters had been assaulted by a male classmate on the school bus! She had been quietly reading her book when the boy went into one of his "states," lashed out, and assaulted her.

I'll spare you my rant about dealing with the politics of a public charter school system, New Jersey and Federal laws, and my discovery of rules that (in my opinion) exist to protect perpetrators and not victims of violence in school. (My fingers are itching to keep typing on that matter, but I'll exert some self-control.)

What I *will* say is that the helpless feeling that my bloody-headed mother felt that day back in my childhood was the same helpless feeling I felt in the pit of my stomach when I saw my daughter's bruised arm. My helplessness quickly turned into a calmed ferocity matched in intensity only with that of a mother belephant whose cub was in danger.

I advocated my ass off behind the scenes on behalf on my daughter, miraculously without cussing out or smacking any of the adults whom I encountered along the way (not to say it did not cross my mind to do so).

I cannot begin to describe how much I disliked that helpless feeling I had as I endeavored to navigate a system that did not display genuine empathy toward my daughter and was more concerned about CYA tactics and following the letter of the law. My inner turmoil was unbearable. I had to keep it together for everyone—for my daughter (so that she had a female mirror who could accurately reflect back her feelings and thoughts to her) and my husband (so that he would not have more than one potential legal matter on his hands, i.e., if mama belephant were to have lashed out or beaten up on anyone).

What almost made me lose it was when the principal (knowing that I was a licensed psychologist trained in treating trauma clients) looked at me across his desk and informed me that he had "consulted with a child psychologist and was recommending that (our daughter) meet with the boy (assailant) for mediation." Assphincter said what!

Something just occurred to me as I'm writing this.

I've had this intense, helpless, frustrated feeling four times with this same daughter: a time in elementary school when a boy hit her, the school bus incident in middle school, and two times in high school when she was nearly hit by a car at a dangerous school-affiliated intersection. No head administrators expressed any genuine interest in her well-being. That makes four times that I felt similar to how my mom likely felt that day when my half-sister Debra beat her up.

I don't know what to make of all this. I feel irate, sad, depressed, ashamed, "postal," helpless, deflated, useless, sickened, paranoid ("What in the universe is seeking to mess up my baby!"), fighting mad (as if I just want to start swinging my fists at any and everything henceforth that even thinks of looking in my baby's direction), etc.

I find that I'm re-examining all of my actions and inactions throughout her life (my brain works like that at times), and I'm questioning if I have done things—this mothering thing—correctly. Have I done what my baby needed (expected) me to do for her? To protect her? To prepare her for the harsh realities of life?

Hmmm.

She knew how to comport herself outside and inside of school and stay focused on her schoolwork.

Tears are welling up in my heart and eyes. My baby girl's acting so . . . much . . . like . . . me.

VIEW FROM THE CHAIR

I cannot enumerate the countless times I've sat across from my female clients who, in the midst of a session, come face-to-face with the stark reality of a seminal pattern in their own life—and the tears begin to flow.

In those moments, the first wave of tears is for themselves as they (for the first time) sit with and feel the pain that they were not allowed/did not have the "luxury" or time to feel or know they had to feel. The second wave of tears usually occurs when they see the effects of those seminal patterns on their children or in another significant interpersonal relationship. If there is a third wave of tears, it is likely due to her thoughts or feelings about what she thinks she can or cannot do to make changes or improvements in the seminal pattern that has surfaced. These moments of facing and feeling the effects of those seminal patterns are never expected.

While every mother or daughter's situation is different—with different histories, dynamics, and dimensions—clinical research and anecdotal therapy findings bear witness that experiencing the first wave of tears places a mother or daughter closer to having compassion for, empathizing with, and advocating for her unmet needs/hopes. This reflection will then provide the basis for her to develop a more informed understanding of her patterns of thoughts, feelings, and reactions in similar situations. The process will also help her clearly see more optimal M–D Relationship Dynamic solutions that take into consideration the thoughts, feelings, and reactions of the others in those similar situations.

(NEW) VIEW FROM THE COUCH

Yes, I grew up in an unsafe home/family environment and even saw and related to the feelings of my mother who struggled to ensure safety in her own family. I internalized her determination. I did not have a shoulder to cry on or a shelter under which I could take refuge. I learned coping skills that helped me maintain a laser focus on my academic and athletic pursuits.

Those life experiences informed me about what I would want to be different for my children. My daughter knew how to

- comport herself outside and in school
- stay focused on her schoolwork and extracurricular activities

Because I parented differently—intentionally—she was also (despite any of our interpersonal difficulties) able to

- come tell me about each of the four occurrences
- feel comfortable expressing her feelings to her daddy and me
- know that she could rest in the fact that her daddy and I had her back

So I must have done something—in this mothering thing—right.

CODE CRACKER

- What expectation have you not communicated to your mother or daughter?

CHAPTER 9
BUSTED RELATIONS

I have a blind spot for how pretty I am. My husband has often had to remind me of my attractiveness not just to him but to other men whom he's seen turn their heads in my direction. Even as I write this, the mention of it makes me feel uncomfortable, and I shrug off the compliment.

My mother was an attractive Jamaican woman with velvet skin, apple cheeks, a stunning smile, and curves in all the right places. Her critical comments about my complexion (especially during pimple-ridden puberty) and my preference for pants (instead of skirts and dresses) and sports (instead of sewing) made me despair of ever meeting her standards. So I stopped trying to put myself together appearance-wise.

I saw my entree to Brown University as the new slate I needed. No one at Brown knew what I was supposed to look like, and individuality was the "in" thing. Awesome for me! So what if my mother only had an eighth-grade education? She raised me in the King's English way of grammar and manners. So what if my mom had aspirations to make it as a seamstress? She and I were one—a team. She was my Trojan, and I was her (academic) workhorse. Our goal: medical school and the higher echelons of economic prosperity. Our ticket: Brown University and a biomedical engineering degree.

Did you catch that? The *bio* covered my major subject preference. The *medical* and *engineering* covered the Jamaican family expectations. (I'd ruled out being a lawyer after watching the movie *The Paper Chase* out of fear of encountering a professor like Professor Kingfield. Go figure. Shows you how my brain was working back then.)

Anyway, the day I left home to drive to Providence, Rhode Island, was the day the clock started ticking. I had eight years to make this dream happen, the first four starting at Brown.

> "DO TWO WALK TOGETHER UNLESS THEY HAVE AGREED TO DO SO?"
> —AMOS 3:3

Psychologist Erik Erikson theorized that a person progresses through the Eight Stages of Psychosocial Development throughout their lifetime.[13] The high school years are when a teenager's sense of self (ego identity) is developing apart from her parents; the teenager explores her values, beliefs, and goals. Brown University's emphasis on student individuality and students pursuing their intellectual passions via its *New Curriculum* was the fertile ground within which I began to find myself—academically, intellectually, socially, and spiritually.

Academically, the hiccup on the road to my medical doctor career plans was organic chemistry. It took me two years (instead of one) to complete it, and with the financial constraint to graduate in four years, the five-year plan was not possible.

Intellectually, my confidence was shot. As a top-ranking student from a competitive, highly-ranked Catholic high school with other top-ranking students from competitive schools, who was I really?

Socially, I mingled well with everyone. I was even elected pledge class president for the Kappa Alpha Theta sorority chapter and served well in that role until I found out how much money I needed to contribute to be able to live in the new sorority chapter's house facility. My work-study jobs just barely kept me afloat each semester, so my sorority life prospects got nixed.

Spiritually, I was a renegade, know-it-all, baptized and confirmed Catholic who'd never read the whole Bible but whose mom had given her a King James Version New Testament (yes, the thees and thous King's English kind). It stayed on a shelf, unopened, in my dorm room.

I never told my mother about all the hurdles and difficulties I was facing during my first two years at Brown. When we would speak every so often on the phone, a typical Miss Communication went as follows:

"Hi, Ma."

"Oh, hi, Booboo. How are you?"

"Fine. How are you, Ma?"

"Okay. Just aches and pains here and there, you know. But still working at that place."

"Oh, okay."

"How are things there with you?"

"They're going. Just working hard."

"That's good. How's Bonnie?" (Bonnie was my freshman-year roommate. Short, bob-cut, blonde-haired, Connecticut-raised, prep-schooled field hockey player with nice parents.)

"She's fine." (Leaving out that I'd decided to join Bonnie and her friends in their drinking sprees for a week and was getting a B in a class instead of an A due to missing a week of classes.)

"I sent you a package in the mail. Make sure to share some with your friends." (My mom's care packages were sweet and thoughtful but included things that were cultural—like grizzada, a delectable coconut and nutmeg pastry—that my peers were not interested in sampling.)

"Thanks, Mom. Well, I gotta go."

"Study hard."

"I am."

"Praying for you."

(Exasperated sigh) "Yes, Mommmm."

I knew my mother was praying for me, but did she have to say that *every* time? I felt like it was her code word or hint to get me to read the Bible. I didn't want to read it; I had too much else to read and study. Plus, in my estimation, any praying she was doing was not working or getting me the kinds of grades I wanted and needed.

My mother and I were not on the same page, spiritually-speaking. She saw God as her solace and friend, someone she could rely on, pray to, and call upon for strength and help in times of trouble. Back in college, I saw God as a distant and uninvolved entity Who had left me to the whims of not-so-nice-people in my own biological family. He also had representatives (priests and nuns) who looked at me and my impoverished state as their mission to help but who would kick me out of Sunday school if I asked earnest questions about God and the Bible. In elementary and high school, I asked such questions because I was trying to make sense of the abused life that I was living, but they showed no interest in getting to know me in *that* context.

My mindset was "What have You done for me lately, God? Nothing. Okay. I'll take care of this myself because I'm by myself." I wasn't outwardly bitter. Well, okay, I was inwardly bitter, and it came out as sarcasm. Still, I just resigned myself to the reality of having to live with the weight and responsibility of doing everything on my own, even if my efforts were not resulting in the exact plans I had for my life.

But what life? When I began to think about those existential questions (Who am I? Why am I here? What is the point of life?)—nothing suicidal, just angsty—I found myself gravitating toward, yup, the Bible. I read it for the first time while I was in college. What I found was a story of a loving Father who loved me so much that He'd sacrifice His only Son, Jesus, for me so that I would not perish but live in relationship with Him forever.

I had an epiphany when I read John 3:16 for the first time. It was as if the words leaped off the page and poured a soothing balm over the deep wounds and crevices of my heart that I had not (consciously) known existed. Could a *father* actually love me that much? I did not deserve it. I could not earn it. He freely gave His all to me because He loved me. All He asked of me was to believe in Him and the gift He provided me in Jesus. The offer was too good to be true. Simply believe? Count me in!

The moment I said yes to this offer in my heart, I was filled with a peace that defied my understanding. Perfect, right? Great news, right? My mom would *definitely* be thrilled to know that I'd finally found God. Well, that He'd found me and answered a prayer that *she'd* been praying as the psalmist had prayed—for God to be a father to the fatherless (Psalm 68:5).

I called my mom.

"Hello?"

"Hi, Ma, it's me."

"Oh, hi, Booboo! How are you? Everything okay?" (I was calling her at a time that was out of the ordinary for me.)

"Yes, Ma. I just wanted you to know that I've accepted Jesus into my heart and I have this incredible peace. I'm so happy."

Silence.

"Ma?"

"Mmm-hmm?"

"Did you hear me?"

"Mmm-hm."

"Well, I can't stay on long. I just wanted to let you know. Thanks for your prayers."

Silence.

As I slowly pulled the phone away from my ear, I felt a bit confused by my mom's reaction. She was the one who had prayed for me and encouraged me to read the blooming Bible to begin with (okay, my sailor mouth was not cleaned up back then). Now here I've given my life to God and Jesus Christ, and she's not happy for me! What's up with that?

That evening, I simmered down and spent the rest of the night into the early morning hours reading the Bible—and my organic chemistry textbook.

My new spiritual path and commitment to God and Jesus soon became a big bone of contention in my relationship with my mom. She had one idea about how I was to live out my spirituality; I had other ideas.

In hindsight, I see that my mom could have found my enthusiastic yet thoughtless recitals of newly memorized Scripture verses and my pontifications about my thoughts on different theological books from the heavy hitters, well, annoying. My mother's simple, soft singing of old hymns and quoting adages based on Bible passages from her childhood memories were constantly at odds with my "what God said" or "what the Bible says" comments.

> **WMNTTD**
>
> ---
>
> As your mom, I like it when you listen to me because it makes me feel that you value me and my experiences.

Even when I physically pointed to the Bible verses that she was speaking about to show her how she might be taking them out of context, she would stiffen up and get more entrenched in her opinion. Similarly, when she would pull the life experience card, stating that I was young and did not know much (and, oh, how I hated when she'd say, "You can have all that book smarts but still be street dumb"), I would just lose it. I'd whine that she "did not understand me" and then go for a drive or end the phone conversation. Oy!

All the years of Miss Conceptions, Miss Understandings from erroneous assumptions, and Miss Communications about my busted boundaries and expectations had laid a shaky foundation for our M–D Relationship. However, prior to her last straw use of the D word, it was this separation from her in my spiritual life decisions that was the first straw adding an undercurrent of strain in our relationship.

Though we prayed to the same God, it didn't feel like we had a common language with which to communicate spiritually.

VIEW FROM THE COUCH

I cringe now when I think about those heated arguments with my mom that ensued after I gave my life to Jesus Christ. My enthusiasm did not speak understanding or respect to my mother. In my happiness, I did not hear the basis for her joy in the midst of her trials and tribulations; I was too busy talking. She never told me about her real struggles; I only saw the outworking of them on her physical well-being. I never told her about my real struggles. She was worn down by the world and too busy living in survival mode to be able to see me, let alone hear about me and my struggles. Gosh! We were like two ships passing in the night (and day).

The busted relationship with my mom made me cling to God tighter as I loosened my desire for control in more areas of my life. My reliance on God ironically made me not only work harder but also smarter—I had more confidence to approach professors for help. One kind psychology professor recognized and affirmed my intellectual prowess and showed me how to balance my time more efficiently. I continue to share those time-management and life-balance skills and insights with my middle school, high school, and collegiate clients as I help them make successful transitions through the different stages of their lives.

Developing and growing into one's sense of self (ego identity) is a bear of a process for *any* teenager. As I think about my daughters—offspring of parents who have high IQs, attended Brown University and M.I.T., and earned their doctoral degrees in the social sciences and engineering—I still have to make an effort to stop and imagine what it must be like for them internally as they are in their junior year of high school. Faced with standardized tests, advanced placement and honors classes, a myriad of letters coming from top and second-tier colleges and universities, and hearing from the adults they encounter "So where do *you* want to go to college?" and "What do *you* plan to major in?"—all this would be enough to make a teenager zone out and not tell anyone anything.

CODE CRACKER

- What do you and your mother or daughter butt heads on?

SECTION TWO
THE REMEDY

One of the things I enjoy about the field of psychology is that (despite sentiments to the contrary) when it comes to practically helping people, psychology is a science. Science is a system of general truths that are obtained from systematic observation and testing using agreed-upon scientific methods. Even though humans are complex and complicated beings, there are common principles derived from centuries of observation which apply to helping improve the human condition.

In my work as a clinical and sport psychologist, the various modes of therapy and performance interventions I use with clients are all predicated on my being able to make a meaningful connection with them. It's in that regard that I rely heavily on principles derived from observations about different attachment styles that people experience in the early years of their development. Psychologists and researchers concur that the type of attachment developed between a child and caregiver (e.g., the M–D Relationship Dynamic) stems from the quality of the *face-to-face interaction* they have with each other. It is this face-to-face (mirroring) process that is key.[14]

This is why Part Two of this book, The Remedy, will make numerous references to mirroring and use the metaphor of mirrors—their formation, damage, and the process for fixing the damage—as the vocabulary for you to find ways to improve your M–D Relationship. Specifically, The Life Mirror Remedy[SM] (which I will refer to throughout this book as The Remedy) for fixing your M–D Relationship will require that you do five key things:

1. Face It (Chapters 10)

2. Clarify It (Chapters 11)

3. Spray It (Chapters 12)

4. Cover It (Chapters 13)

5. Engage It (Chapters 14–15)

PART 4
THE FIX
FIRST FOUR KEYS

"I like mirrors because they suggest the sense of going beyond appearances."

—Claude Chabrol, quoted in
The Late Films of Claude Chabrol
French Director

CHAPTER 10
FACE IT[SM]

The first key to fixing the rifts (cracks) in your M–D Relationship is to Face It. When you encounter a mirror for the first time, it is best to look at what you see. As simple as it sounds, it's not always the easiest thing to do.

A petite, well-dressed woman named Paula came to my office one early evening. She had come to me to get help for dealing with anxiety issues that had been causing her distress in multiple areas of her life. I expressed to Paula how much courage it took for her to seek out help and that I was committed to working with her through the problems that plagued her.

She expressed that her anxiety was occurring when she had to give presentations to colleagues at her job. I intently listened to her, giving her my full, undivided attention, empathizing with any and every feeling she emoted via my countenance and reflective choice of words in response to her. After listening to her recount various instances of heightened anxiety, I conducted a comprehensive mental health assessment and asked her additional questions regarding her family of origin and her past work experiences/environments. It was during that time of inquiry that Paula offhandedly mentioned a time in middle school when she had experienced humiliation from her peers.

At the conclusion of the assessment, I shared my thoughts with Paula.

> **Me:** "It looks like your current anxiety happens under these particular conditions, which I can help you address one at a time through EMDR Therapy.[15] However, I believe the underlying root cause of your anxiety stems back to your middle school experience with your peers, and EMDR Therapy can address that also."

Paula's body stiffened. She blinked.

> **Paula (retorting):** "That middle school stuff has nothing to do with my anxiety now."

> **Me:** "I hear you, Paula. We can address the current circumstances contributing to your anxiety, and that's fine. I do think, however, that addressing that past middle school event will get at the root of what is making the current circumstances so bothersome for you."

Paula blinked again.

> **Paula:** "I want to address the current circumstances."

For me, as a clinician, my ultimate focus is to help my clients by connecting with them where they are. Paula was in her current circumstances. However, clinically I knew that (specifically for Paula's situation) merely addressing her current circumstances would lengthen her time in therapy.

She'd go from one problem to the next, to the next—and so on—without taking full ownership for her contribution(s) or solutions to her situations.

I also knew that everything is connected, and eventually the middle school event would come up. So, instead of what could've been a four-month-long treatment process if my initial observations and treatment recommendations had been heeded, it was eight months later when the middle school event eventually re-surfaced in our session. Once it was addressed, the other areas in Paula's life began to shift toward emotional healing.

In math—one of the universal languages—there is a geometry theorem that says the shortest distance between two points is a straight line. Colloquially-speaking, that sentiment is expressed as "cut to the chase" or "get to the point." Yet, it seems that we as human beings usually take a different tact with regard to addressing issues in our lives. We go around the crux of the matter instead of just facing things head-on.

In Section 1 (The Rifts), I led you through my personal journey of things I have had to face looking into the mirror of my life (as a daughter raised by a single mom, a mom of twin daughters, and a licensed psychologist).

Now, in Section 2 (The Remedy), I invite you to follow me through a process (framework) that I've developed to help you fix the rifts in your M–D Relationship.

Since this book is *not* intended to be a long treatise on mother–daughter interactions, I will be taking the shortest route possible to explain what will improve your M–D Relationship.

TAKE A LOOK AT YOUR HEART

I think Phil Collins was onto something when he belted the chorus of "Against All Odds," which speaks of someone's anguished realization that he has nothing but memories of a relationship instead of the real-time physical closeness of one. I've always imagined him singing that song with an agonized face, ripping his shirt to bare his chest, showing his take-a-look-at-me-now vulnerability as he admits the real state of his heart in that moment.

As you prepare to embark on this portion of The Remedy process, consider this question: What is the remedy for an M–D Relationship that has cracks or that is shattered?

The answer: Love.

In certain circles of the psychological world, the concept of love is described as giving someone "unconditional positive regard" or being "*person*-centered." No matter what you call it, though, love is that one thing that makes the biggest difference in relationships, whether it is between spouses, siblings, platonic peer friendships, or a mother and daughter. This love is not the mushy, eyelid flapping, romantic kind of love (*eros*), nor is it the brotherly/sisterly kind of love (*phileo*). The unconditional positive regard that is person-centered and to which I'm referring is the kind of love (*agape*) that

- has no strings attached

- is freely given

- is primarily desirous for the good of someone else while still being true to the core essence of who you know yourself to be

I'd like to ask you to pause for moment and consider the following question: What's the state of your heart when it comes to loving your daughter or mother?

THE DOWNWARD DONUT

Preparation

For me, love (the *agape* kind) was my aspiration on the day when, on a tight schedule, I decided to squeeze in some quality time with our youngest twin daughter, Jasmine. Though tired and exasperated with the then-tense M–D dynamics in our relationship, I was excited to try something different. I'd suggested a Saturday trip to her favorite donut establishment for some sit-down time just so I could listen more to her (and talk less).

Saturday afternoon came. I got my wallet and car keys and walked into the dining room where Jasmine was sitting. She was studying—*and eating*. In a low soft voice, I asked, "Are you ready to go? It's 3:00 p.m." She looked at me with a blank, deer-in-the-headlights stare.

Jasmine: "Go where?"

Me: "To Dunkin Donuts. You'd said you wanted to go to Dunkin Donuts."

Jasmine: "Uh, I did?"

Me (with slumped shoulders): "Yes, you did."

Jasmine: "I have (school) work to do."

At that moment, something inside me cracked. *Phssssssssssss sssssssssssssssss.* All the air in my sail left me—in a world of hurt.

A myriad of thoughts raced through my mind: *How could she do that? She agreed earlier this week that she was committing to these trips in an effort to lay new groundwork for us. This would help us get a more stable footing in our tense relationship and move on into establishing new patterns with each other.*

(Wrong) Implementation
The rest of what happened next became an out-of-body, slow-motion, *Matrix*-like experience. (Warning: Do *not* try this at home.)

I heard myself:

1. Interrogate: asking her questions about her thought process when she'd originally agreed to go with me

2. Interrogate: asking her questions about what she had actually been doing with her time for the past two hours when she was supposedly doing school work (with the TV on and chatting with her sister)

3. Explicate: expressing why and how much I'd been looking forward to getting together with her

4. Guilt-Inflict: whiningly informing her about how I'd changed my whole schedule around to take this trip with her

5. Rehash: bringing up material from past interactions that had nothing to do with the present interaction (in this particular instance, monetary issues)

Jasmine's blank stare, one-word answers, and "I don't know" responses felt as if salt were being rubbed into old wounds of rejection and dismissal from the ghosts in my past. I tried to regroup and recover, and then I heard myself summarily state: "Well, I hear that you don't want to go to Dunkin Donuts with me, that you'd forgotten about our scheduled outing, and that you have a lot of schoolwork to do. I had really looked forward to spending time with you."

And with that, I left the room and went to go sit on the couch in our family room. Though I sat there on the couch, channel surfed, and eventually landed on a sports channel, the surfing continued in my mind and heart.

Realization
I saw mirror images of my mother slaving wearily over things— cooking, cleaning, sewing up rips in clothing to make it last

longer—while I scampered along in my child/teen world, taking for granted all that she was doing to keep things going. She did all these things for me not because I asked her to, not because I expected her to, definitely not because "that's what mothers do" (remember, she chose not to throw me into a garbage can!). My mom did all those things *out of her love for me*.

In a different way at that particular moment, I realized that a mother's love is a choice, and in the execution of that choice, sometimes mothers will get (or feel) hurt. I'd felt hurt.

Having this small rift occur in my interactions with Jasmine—a Miss Conception, Miss Understanding, and Miss Communication about what we were going to be doing that Saturday and why—I had to face three uncomfortable facts:

1. I had not emotionally and mentally prepared properly for the outing.

2. I had implemented the dynamics of our interaction incorrectly.

3. I came to my realizations too late to have prevented my incorrect implementations.

Here is what I should have done:

1. had more realistic conceptions (hopes) of what would transpire during our outing (properly preparing emotionally and mentally)

2. implemented dynamics more appropriately by adjusting my behavior and not overcompensating (immediately barraging her with interrogative questions to "get a better understanding" while I was feeling so hurt)

3. communicated better by listening more

Oh, that things would go so perfectly! Instead, it was *messy*. I *felt* bad. But my main point is not about the mess and how I felt. Messy, bad stuff happens often; what's important is *how you respond* to it. That's what really matters.

What do you do when your mirror gets cracked? Do you walk away and find another mirror? While that is a plausible option—one that we all opt for at times—the subtle ramifications are many.

One of those ramifications is that your avoidance of that cracked mirror will result in a daily habit of not frequenting that particular space or area of your home (your daughter or mother's life), therefore limiting your mobility (your M–D Relationship progress).

The more optimal choice is to *face* the consequences of the rift by doing three things:

- **Preparing** to have a mirror held up to you regarding your actions/inaction in the situation

- **Implementing** a course of action that incorporates information that you've learned about yourself from that mirror

- **Realizing** that any corrections you attempt to make in light of the realization you've had will be imperfectly perfect if you are sincerely attempting to address the issues

For Jasmine, her preparation came from her considering the words of a sage adult family friend whose advice helped her see and take ownership for the effect her actions were having on others, including me. For me, the preparation came in a different form.

The day after our downward donut rift occurred, I dodged

church (and, ironically, the sermon on love that had been on the schedule) because I just couldn't deal with people that day. Instead, I chose to mope around in a bookstore. After wandering through the main aisles, I stumbled upon Steven Covey's book, *The 7 Habits of Highly Effective Families*.[16] When I flipped open the book, the pages opened to his chapter on Habit 5: "Seek First to Understand, Then to Be Understood."

As I read, it was as if every word of that chapter levitated to reach my face and then stayed there, floating before me—facing me. I was jettisoned back to my elementary school days at St. Mary's in the Bronx as the hymnals were opened and the priest led us to sing St. Francis of Assisi's "Make Me a Channel of Your Peace." The words "grant that I may never seek so much . . . to be understood as to understand" rang through my head and traveled the 18 inches toward my heart.

(Corrected) Implementation

Just as that lyric sank into my heart, my cell phone vibrated. It was a text message from Jasmine. Here is the text exchange that followed:

Jasmine: I'm sorry I wasn't much help yesterday during our conversation . . . It was a lot of information to take in, and I felt pretty inhuman and sad afterward, so that's why I was crying/being quiet . . . I just don't feel like talking about it today. *(Taking ownership. Explaining.)*

Me: I too am VERY sorry for not hearing you and over-loading you with everything. *(Taking Ownership. Specific Apology.)*

Jasmine: It's fine. *(Acceptance.)*

Me: I so want to understand you (from your perspective), and I feel like I'm not giving you what you need. I'm also sorry that I've not been hearing/listening to you . . . (it's not intentional) . . . I just need to get better at that too. *(Taking ownership. Specific apology. Genuine heart expressions.)*

Jasmine: It's fine . . . I just won't ask you guys for much anymore unless it's the basic essentials because then I'll feel bad and feel like I'm using you guys for your money when I'm trying not to.

Me: I am also sorry for saying things that have made you feel that way. I know you are not using us for money. And I understand how you might think that, given stuff I've said . . . I hear that you feel hurt, misunderstood, and frustrated. *(Specific apology. Affirmation of the other's heart. Taking ownership.)*

Jasmine: Yeah. Pretty much . . . *sighs*

Me: I am VERY sorry.

Jasmine: I hear you.

Me: I don't know what to do. I will give you whatever space you need. Just please know that I love you VERY much and am & will be here for you in whatever capacity you need &/or are able to tell me. *(Affirmation. Honest heart expression. Unconditional positive regard expressed.)*

Jasmine: Okay.

Me: If you can receive a virtual hug from me . . . I humbly offer it to you. If you are not able to receive a virtual hug from me, that's okay. A virtual or real one will be there whenever you need it. *(Unconditional positive regard expressed.)*

Jasmine: Okay.

When Jasmine and I saw each other later that day, she was not open to receive any hug from me. I had to be (and was) okay with her decision because that was where she was emotionally and relationally. I had to (and did) respect her and her space.

A few days later, as she was heading to her room to go to bed, she reached out to me for a goodnight hug.

VIEW FROM THE COUCH

Realizations

The process of addressing a rift in mother–daughter dynamics is not a neat and tidy process. It's messy. Mostly, I'm up for the challenge of making the necessary corrections. I have to admit, though, that going from the toddler and elementary-school years to the middle-school and high-school years has been a challenge—not just for me, but I'm sure for my daughters, too.

Early on, it seemed like the rift-repair process was more straightforward: a rift would occur and I'd take ownership for my role in it and apologize. I had no expectation of either daughter's ability or capacity to be introspective enough to take a similar degree of ownership and express an insightful, heartfelt apology.

But when they entered the teen years (one stage away from young adulthood), my expectations shifted. I expected them to be introspective enough to readily (a.k.a. speedily) apologize to me. I began "feeling some kinda way" about their apparent inattention to the effects of their actions on others, including me—their mother. I soon found myself taking longer to apologize to them (three hours instead of three minutes).

> **WMNTTD**
>
> As your mom, the biggest risk I take everyday is to unconditionally love you while not knowing if you will ever love me back the same way (unconditionally).

It was the downward donut debacle with Jasmine that jolted me into remembering that, regardless of her age, *I* am still the adult—the older adult—in the M–D Relationship. *I* need to be the adult who is raising and guiding my daughter toward adulthood. It is imperative for me to choose to *model* mature adult behavior for her out of my love for her. Period.

My responsibility as a mom is to choose. As Chatham Sullivan noted in *The Clarity Principle*, "The primary responsibility of [someone in a leadership role—e.g., a mother] . . . is to take responsibility. Choice . . . must be formed from the leader's ability to *own the burden* that accompanies power. . . . When we [moms] embrace choice, we gain clarity of purpose. . . . clarity attracts . . ."[17] (emphasis added).

It is this attraction that facilitates mothers and daughters connecting in ways that become beneficial for daughters in the long run.

VIEW FROM THE CHAIR

Psychologists and social scientists have long studied the mother–daughter relationship and have concluded that it has a significant impact on the mental and emotional well-being of daughters during the teenage years.[18] Additionally, those researchers have found that for M–D Relationships, the degree of mother–daughter connectedness (the ability of mothers and daughters to share their feelings and ideas which is indicative of their having a healthy emotional attachment to each other) positively predicts the level of self-esteem in adult daughters. In short, a healthy mother–daughter connection helps daughters develop a high level of self-esteem when they become adults.

Interestingly, these studies have also found that the degree of advice-taking behavior and help-seeking behavior regarding emotional and practical issues by daughters in the M–D Relationship had a *negative* effect on an adult daughter's self-esteem. So an M–D Relationship that has a dynamic in which a daughter is repeatedly looking to her mom for advice or help (and her mom is not allowing her daughter to take the opportunity to either figure things out on her own or attempt to "do for herself") is actually doing the daughter a disservice in the long run.

CRACKING THE CODE

According to various glass repair websites,[19] the process of fixing a small crack in a mirror involves

1. **Preparing** the mirror surface by cleaning it with a soft cloth to clear off any dirt

2. **Implementing** the fix by applying a stabilizer (film covering) over the crack or a resin (a viscous adhesive material) to the crack and letting the combination cure (harden—solidify with time)

3. **Removing** the stabilizer film covering

Similarly, this process can serve as a framework for fixing small rifts in your M–D Relationship.

1. **Preparation:** Prepare your mirror surface first by

   a. Cleaning your heart with love

   b. Clearing your VOICE: Finding your **Venue Of Interaction Chosen for Engagement** with your mother or daughter (for example, schedule a time to be together or engage in an activity that the other person would enjoy or which would be conducive to facilitating the bonding process)

2. **Implementation:** Implement the fix by

a. Applying the stabilizer of stopping and taking stock: taking a hard look at the dynamics of and triggers in your M–D Relationship

b. Applying the resin of

  i. Taking ownership: Take responsibility for your contribution to the current dynamics.

  ii. Understanding: Purpose to try to understand where your mom or daughter is coming from and put yourself in her shoes for a minute (this is called empathizing).

c. Allowing time for your insights to cure before implementing any new behaviors or approaches. Give things time to solidify within your heart and mind; the length of time differs for everyone.

3. **Realization:** Remove the stabilizer film covering. Realizations are like removing a film from one's eyes. Own up to where you are lacking in love regarding your actions; this is the key to facing yourself in the mirror. Such foundational realizations will help cement the bond fixes in your M–D Relationship.

Working through this process of Preparation, Implementation, and Realization helps mothers and daughters face what's going on within themselves and in each other.

CODE CRACKER

- How (or in what area) are you lacking in empathy towards your mother or daughter?

CHAPTER 11

CLARIFY IT℠

In Chapter 10, we looked at how to Face It: face what's going on within yourself, your daughter/mother, and your M–D Relationship Dynamics. The second key in The Remedy is to Clarify It. After you look at yourself in the mirror, it is not uncommon to see things you hadn't noticed before and take steps to spruce up whatever you consider not to be up-to-snuff. Similarly, when addressing small rifts/cracks in an M–D Relationship, you may notice bigger issues that require more clarification.

It's kind of like peeling back an onion—there may or may not be some crying involved. But when the peeling is done and the pieces are added to the food of your life, it can add a savory flavoring that permeates all aspects of it and makes it taste *good*.

Now, you may have jumped to this—The Remedy—section of the book when you read its title in the table of contents in the hope of bypassing prior material so you can address the big cracks/rifts in your M–D Relationship. I commend you for your desire to take the straightest route to a solution, and I admire your heart and tenacity to get to the root of the matter quickly. I get it—you're tired of the mess, ruin, or rubble that exists between the two of you. I would ask, though, that you consider what I'm about to share about a commercial.

A JOB DONE

I did a Job Squad paper towel commercial when I was in middle school. Having grown up in a tattered South Bronx apartment, I was accustomed to bathrooms and kitchens that had chipped, lead-infused painted walls and rusty pipes. Now, with this commercial, I would experience the cleaner side of life within the images portrayed on TV.

My role in the Job Squad commercial was to be an industrious young girl who was cleaning a bathtub and a kitchen window. Having just finished shooting a Macy's and Bamberger's retail store commercial on location, I was excited to see where this more domestically-themed commercial would be filmed.

When I arrived at the studio location, I was escorted to wardrobe and makeup. I was a tad disappointed to be working in a studio, but I still remained upbeat about being able to clean something using this product.

Now, this is not to disparage Job Squad or its customers, but the next set of events shocked me. Instead of filming me cleaning really dirty tiles or windows, the director first filmed me cleaning *clean* (lightly soiled) tiles and windows!

"Lights! Camera! *Action!*"

There I stood, staring into the camera, saying my lines, and wiping a neatly folded sheet of Job Squad across a barely-soiled surface. We went through take after take. The director wanted my hand placed *just so* and my wiping motion *just so*. When that part of the shoot was done, I was given a break and lunch back in my dressing room. When the next round of filming was set to start, I was escorted back into the studio.

As I walked closer to the set this time, I was dumbstruck. The lightly soiled tile and window surfaces were now *filthy*. My role during this segment was to stand in the midst of this mess and say my lines that expressed my befuddlement at how I would *ever* get such a dirty space clean. Take after take ensued; the director wanted me to "capture the emotions" of feeling overwhelmed, concerned, and helpless about the mess. I was asked to convey to my viewing audience how it would feel to be a daughter whose mother expected her to clean it all and the emotions of relief and hope that such a task would now be possible because of my decision to use Job Squad paper towels!

Wait. Can I put an LOL here? I've got a chuckle welling up inside me as I recall the kinds of things I was asked to do as a child actress.

Okay, now I've caught my breath from my LOL moment.

This paper towel was going to "save" me. It was going to help me deal with the mess in front of me, save my expenditure of time and effort, and help me meet the expectations of my actress mom (who was to commend me for a "job well done"). That's what I was to sell to my audience. Quick work with less time and effort—and I could address my M–D Relationship to boot!

The kicker for me was that, in the commercial, we filmed the *result* first and I never got to work through the messy cleaning process with the product. Unbeknownst to me, I contributed to the perpetuation of the illusion that getting things clean is easy.

Messages like "cleaning is easy" have seeped into how many mothers and daughters approach their M–D Relationship. They just want things to be clean and effortless—now.

Well, M–D Relationships are messy. Period.

Mothers have dreams of being close with their daughters—sharing similar interests, engaging in bonding activities, having meaningful talks, etc. Daughters are consciously and unconsciously taking in their mom's likes, dislikes, mannerisms, and particularities. However, once daughters enter what I call the first wave of the separation-individuation process as a toddler, the proverbial tug-of-war begins as they endeavor to separate, to become their own person, and to develop their own identity.

While this tug-of-war is occurring with and within their daughters, mothers are experiencing their own tug-of-war. They are dealing not only with the current tugs/rifts/conflicts/tensions with their daughters but also with the tugs of the past that they experienced—and may still be experiencing—as a daughter with their mother. Whew! There's a whole lot of tugging going on!

It's enough to make a person want to curl up under a blanket—or go shopping.

In her book *You're Grounded Forever . . . But First Let's Go Shopping*, Susan Shapiro Barash observed how mothers and daughters seem to view the activity of shopping together as the panacea for fostering mother–daughter closeness.[20] In actuality, shopping only provides a barely soiled surface for the Job Squad paper towels to clean.

If mothers and daughters don't accept the fact that improving their relationship with each other is a messy process, then the process will be flat-out frustrating. Additionally, the bigger the mess (crack/rift), the more involved the cleaning process will be.

But first, what is the purpose of cleaning a mirror? Is it not to rid it of dirt, scum, and grime? Such goals for cleanliness are admirable. But as we continue on this journey to address the big(ger) cracks/rifts in your M–D Relationship, I'd ask for you to consider that the dirt, scum, and grime may actually serve a purpose.

DIRTLESS TO (ALMOST) TOOTHLESS

I went to a local physical therapist's office last year. It was my first time at the new facility. I walked through the front doors of the building to enter a spacious waiting room that was separated from the physical therapy (PT) room by a very clean floor-to-ceiling glass wall and set of doors. I entered the workroom and had an engaging conversation with the physical therapist, named Bradford.

At the conclusion of our talk, we both got up and moved toward the doors leading back into the waiting room. As we kept talking, I said something funny and we both began to laugh. Still laughing, I shook Bradford's hand, thanked him for his time, whirled around, and took a step.

BAM!

I jolted backward and fell to the floor.

I had just walked smack into the clean glass door.

I had not seen it. It was as clear as glass comes. That was all I could gather as my head spun and Bradford checked me out for immediate concussive symptoms (though, being a sport psychologist, I was aware that I did not have any).

A few minutes into the aftermath and one ice pack later, Bradford apologetically explained how I was not the only person who'd done a similar head-first move into the glass door. "I've talked to our management about getting some type of decal put on the glass," he told me.

When I returned to the PT office a few weeks later for my first official visit, there were very large decals on the glass panels and glass doors. It made a *huge* difference, from a not-doing-another-header-into-the-glass-door perspective.

The presence of some kind of dirt (decal) on the clear glass made me realize that there *can* be a benefit in an M–D Relationship not being so clean or clear all the time. Those Decals of Difference™ can help each person in the relationship not run into things and get hurt. Decals of Difference can help us see where we are and where we ought or ought not to be going in our M–D Relationship, which can help guide us in our pursuit of improving our mother–daughter dynamics.

So, now that we've taken some time to lay the groundwork for addressing M–D Relationships and have clarified some matters, let's look at things in more detail. Specifically, we are going to go a tad bit deeper and look at the process of clarifying the bigger cracks/rifts in your M–D Relationship. As we shall see in Chapters 12 and 13, this clarifying process will involve spraying and covering—the third and fourth keys of The Remedy, respectively.

CHAPTER 12
SPRAY IT^{SM}

The third key in The Remedy is to Spray It. This involves delving deeper to get more clarity about the interactions you have with your daughter or mother and the effect you each have on the other.

At the risk of sounding like a clean freak, I'm going to tell you something about our bathroom. When we lived in New Jersey, we had a 1,800-square-foot bi-level home in a quiet suburban neighborhood. Our master bedroom was small, and our master bathroom was even smaller. It had a standing shower stall, toilet, and one sink atop a box-shaped vanity and a recessed mirrored cabinet in the wall above it. All this was to be shared by me—a 5-foot-6-inch woman—and my 6-foot-2-inch, burly-chested BFF hubby.

We made do for the 14 years we lived there. We had a rhythm in our use of that one vanity and mirror. And when it got dirty, we both cleaned it. When we watched home-buying

TV shows, we'd wonder with baffled looks, "Why on earth is that couple making such a fuss over having a double vanity in the master bathroom?"

Well, when we moved into our 2,800-square-foot, two-story North Carolina home in a quiet rural neighborhood development, we were stunned when we saw that our home had a master bathroom with a double vanity! After being in our home a little over two years at the writing of this book, I can say that I simply *love* having a double vanity! Those home-buying TV couples were onto something (just kidding . . . not kidding . . .).

Okay. All kidding aside for a moment, though. Now that we do have a double vanity, one of the things I've noticed is the state of each mirror above our respective sinks. My mirror tends to have less toothpaste splatter than my husband's mirror. Granted, we both clean the double vanity for each other, but I've found that *my* tolerance for the elapsed time in-between cleanings is shorter than his. I love my BFF hubby, so please don't read anything into this other than me noticing that we are different in this way.

Our bathroom mirrors got me thinking about how we all go through our days, weeks, and years going in and out of our bathrooms. We do our daily hygienic rituals, not paying too much attention to the way in which the spray of our vanity activities leaves a trail of scum and mess in our wake. What we are left with is a sprayed mirror in which it becomes hard to see our real reflection—unless we regularly clean the mirror.

This is similar to the way things in our life—our early childhood experiences, peer relationships, life experiences, etc.—spray scum and dirt onto what I call our Life Mirror. The remnants of dirt, scum, and fog are the scripts that are splattered on that mirror, and this becomes the imperfect lens through which we see our reflection.

If you are a mom reading this book, then know that you are bringing *your* Life Mirror to your M–D Relationship. If you are a daughter reading this book, then what your mom has sprayed onto your Life Mirror so far is *some* of what you bring to your M–D Relationship with her.

The third key of The Remedy—Spray It—(metaphorically) refers to your attending to what's been sprayed onto your personal Life Mirror. That attending will involve

1. assessing how clean or dirty your Life Mirror is

2. identifying your goal(s) for cleaning your Life Mirror

3. determining what to use—another spray or something else—to clean your Life Mirror

Now, let's take a look at these three parts.

PART 1: HOW CLEAN OR DIRTY IS YOUR MIRROR?

Please know that I'm not trying to impose my own cleaning preferences onto you. I *am* wondering, though, when was the last time you looked at your bathroom mirror? I'm not talking about a casual glance but an intentional, *real* look at your bathroom mirror. Sometimes we are so focused on other things in life that we can find it hard to examine this item. So take a moment now to go to your bathroom and take a look at your mirror. I'll wait.

(I'm humming the *Jeopardy* game show theme as I check out my own bathroom mirror now.)

Okay, you're back? Great!

Now, when you got to your bathroom mirror, what did you do?

I ask the question "What did you *do?*" instead of "What did you *find?*" because I've noticed that most of the time when we go in front of a mirror, the first thing we do is look at *ourselves* and not the mirror. We are drawn in by what we see of ourselves in the mirror. We also quickly take action to make adjustments to our face, body, clothing, or makeup, etc. We rarely look at the mirror that is providing us with the reflected information. The mirror draws us in and focuses our attention on us, and then reactions get stirred up within us. We can get so engrossed in ourselves—our appearance, our imperfections—that we sometimes lose sight of larger external factors in our midst.

So, what *did* you find?

Jot down or note your finding(s) here: _____
_____.

Now, let me suggest that instead of reacting to the reflection of our present self which we see in the mirror, wouldn't it make sense to take stock of the mirror itself that is reflecting us, not in a judgmental but in an understanding way? After all, if there is something "not just right" or "a little off" with the mirror, or if something on the mirror is "blocking the view," then wouldn't it make sense to attend to those items first?

While that *would* make sense, something keeps us from checking out the very source of the reflection information that we are relying on for feedback about ourselves. Sometimes, it's the fact that the bathroom mirror tends to be big, and if there is a smudge of some sort, we can usually maneuver ourselves around it to get a general sense of our reflection. Sometimes, it's the fact that the mirror is small, and if there's a smudge, we just do a mental guesstimation of what our image is supposed to look like. Whether we have a big or small mirror, it's simply human nature to make adjustments to bring us to a place or state of equilibrium, comfort, and ease. Having to address the mirror itself would require more effort.

When I went a moment ago to examine my bathroom mirror, I found some light smudges and lint in various sections. I have *no* idea how some of those splatterings could've gone so high! Still, I mentally noted it—and moved onto the next task that I deemed more important (writing this book). So the smudges and lint will continue to build up over time. I know I won't let it go more than a week before I clean it, though. Again, that's just me.

How clean or dirty is *your* personal mirror—your Life Mirror? Here are some things to for you to consider.

If you are a mother, you may want to consider the following three types of sprays that may be building up on your Life Mirror:

1. In what ways or instances do you feel *unappreciated* or underappreciated by your daughter?

2. What things do you do that you believe go *unnoticed* by your daughter?

3. What aspects of you/your life do you feel your daughter is *uninterested* in?

Think about and/or write down your answers to those questions. What are the themes of the sentiments, and when are you repeatedly saying those things to your daughter? If your daughter is really young (less than six years old), think about when you've expressed such sentiments to your spouse or friend.

If you are a daughter, you may want to consider the following three types of sprays from your mom that may be building up on your Life Mirror:

1. What *reaction* does your mother generally have toward you?

2. What *expectations* (verbalized and not verbalized) does your mother have of you?

3. In what ways or circumstances do you feel *devalued* by your mother?

Think about and/or write down what feelings and reactions you have in each of those spray moments. What are you doing with those feelings and reactions?

Each of your answers to these questions will provide you with insight into what may be contributing to the current dynamics occurring and what scripts you are likely spraying within and throughout your M–D Relationship.

VIEW FROM THE CHAIR

For the most part, baby girls have their mom (or some other significant female caregiver) as their first mirror. A mother's face is a baby daughter's first mirror that reflects back to her what she is experiencing internally and externally. All the face-to-face cooing, cuddling, eye contact, and the like are dynamics that occur between a mother and daughter early on in a daughter's psychosocial, mental, and emotional development.[21] These mother–daughter interactions form the foundational basis through which daughters gain

- a sense of the world around them (is the world safe or unsafe?)

- feedback about their own needs (are others validating and/or responsive to my needs or not?)

- validation of their own abilities (can I confidently take steps toward autonomy and independence and be successful or not?)

- affirmation of their own worth as a person and rela-tional being (are others desirous to be around and interact with me or not?)

That significant caregiver—a baby girl's mother—is bigger than life in the daughter's eyes. Mom is the main source of her care, nourishment, social information, and affirmation/ validation. A girl sees herself in her mom; the two are one. So when a baby girl cries and her mom responds with "Awwww" and comforts her, she learns that what she experienced in her world is accurate and true. If a baby has a bowel movement in her diaper and her mother changes it in a timely fashion, she learns that the weird-feeling-thing (a.k.a. poo) that just came out of her is not meant to stay on her bottom but is to be wiped away. These lessons get translated and logged into a baby girl's mind and body as a script for what happens when she cries or defecates. Similarly, such scripts get formed within a daughter as she progresses through the years and the interactions with and feedback from her mother increase and change at the various stages of her development.

A former client of mine, Barbara, who had come to see me for anxiety-related issues, once shared a story with me. As a middle-schooler, every time she'd speak up to defend her younger brother, her mother would chastise her for "being aggressive like a man." This early childhood spray on her Life Mirror led her to think (as a 56-year-old woman) that speaking up is not ladylike.

For years in her corporate career, Barbara had difficulty making product presentations in front of men and would then get frustrated that she was not being promoted. She had spent a bit of time in therapy avoiding examining the mirror in her life—her mom—and, instead, focused on her own shortcomings. She adjusted her current thoughts, feelings, and behaviors to alleviate her presentation anxiety symptoms. With that approach, Barbara had made progress in feeling better about her presentation skills.

However, no significant change occurred in Barbara's ability to move forward toward new interpersonal relationship dynamics with her adult daughter until she was able to examine—in a compassionate, understanding way—her mom and the scripts that she had sprayed onto her Life Mirror.

PART 2: WHAT IS YOUR MIRROR-CLEANING GOAL?

Depending on what you found on your own bathroom mirror, you're probably either sighing with resignation about having to add yet another cleaning task to your list of things to do or you're sighing with relief about *not* having to add yet another cleaning task to your list. Maybe you did not check your bathroom mirror and are deciding to postpone the examination until later. Or maybe you've decided that you are not going to be bothered to look at anything mirror-related at this point in time. (I hope this is not the case for you, but I understand if it is. That's okay for now. I want you to know that I applaud your honesty and I am sincerely glad that you've read this far in this book. I also appreciate your sticking with it.)

Whenever you decide to examine your bathroom mirror—your Life Mirror—it's important to determine what your goal will be for cleaning it. Remember, your goals are influenced by your expectations. As we covered in Chapters 1–3, when a mother has an unmet expectation, she can become prone to overcompensate to mask over the internal emotional pain of having had a Miss Conception about her situation. This can lead to her having Miss Understandings and Miss Communications in her M–D Relationship.

Having a goal that you expect to be able to attain can result in you taking definitive actions toward it; having a goal that you do *not* really expect to reach is likely to result in you not taking any definitive actions to obtain it.

Your expectations for cleaning mirrors may be different from the next mother's or daughter's, and that's okay. The important thing to remember is that your goals are exactly that—*your* goals. And your goals are important.

Windex to the Rescue?

The whole mirror-cleaning-goals thing reminds me of when I was a tween and spent two days filming a Windex commercial.

"Wipe off the grime and cheer up . . . put on a Windex shine." This was the jingle for that cleaning product. The marketing campaign promoted the idea that shine = clean and you could put on a shine just by wiping off the grime which, in turn, would make you feel better.

That "wipe, shine, feel better" mindset has seeped into M–D Relationships. Mothers and daughters expect that their relationships are to shine—have this appearance of being smooth and unblemished.[22] So, with that expectation, many mothers and daughters make it their goal to keep things going smoothly by wiping over any imperfections and blemishes in their M–D Relationships. They'll do this by

- *abdicating responsibility* for their actions or inactions
- *minimizing* conflict
- *ignoring* glaring tensions
- *stuffing* their real feelings
- *sugar-coating* their real thoughts

Having a Windex-like approach can be counterproductive for your cleaning goal expectations and hazardous to your M–D Relationship health. So what's a mom or daughter to do? It's okay. Just keep your eyes on your mirror-cleaning goal.

What is your goal for cleaning your Life Mirror? Think about or jot your answer down here:

My goal for having a clean(er) Life Mirror is

_____

_____

_____

It is possible that although you have the above-listed goal for cleaning your Life Mirror, you may have to consider using different methods depending on what you want the result to look like.

PART 3: OH, THE PLACES YOU COULD GO . . . WITH DIFFERENT OPTIONS!

If your goal is to clean your Life Mirror, then there are several options.

The first of these options involves the use of manufactured products: chemicals that remove dirt, soap scum, and stains but affect a host of other areas of your personal and global environment. For example, the original Windex formula had combustible ingredients that stripped dirt, scum, and grime off window and mirror surfaces and made them shiny but *not* clean.[23] Relationally-speaking, this would be equivalent to a mother or daughter doing the following:

- Using a technique or doing something just to do it. The interpersonal dynamics occur in a mechanistic way to rectify the relationship between a mother and daughter, but the intervention itself is devoid of any natural flow or genuineness.

- Using interventions that are well-intentioned but may not be coming from a place of clear self-awareness and understanding, which could potentially do more damage than good.

Overall, these approaches may make the surface of an M–D Relationship look shiny, but they do not *really* clean it.

A second option for cleaning mirrors involves the use of natural liquid products (vinegar, ammonia, rubbing alcohol, water, etc.) that break up particles of dirt, soap scum, and stains naturally. These products primarily address getting things clean without a shine, and they cost less to your wallet and the surrounding environment. Relationally-speaking, this natural option is akin to digging deep to apply principles more organically in the moment within your M–D Relationship.

For example, one of my consulting clients, Amber, recounted how one Friday morning her daughter had woken up on the wrong side of the bed and was grumpy and snippy at anyone in her proximity—and that "anyone" was Amber. Amber said that she just let her daughter vent, having noticed that she had stayed up late for several nights to study for a test that was scheduled for that day. The next day, Saturday, Amber cooked a full breakfast for her family and left her late-rising daughter a special, sectioned-off amount of food just for her. Later in the day, without any prompting, Amber's daughter apologized for her previous inconsiderate behavior.

Before consulting with me, Amber would have quipped back at her daughter about her lack of sensitivity to others in the family and how she needed to mind her attitude. However, after I helped Amber work through and attend to her own Life Mirror, she began to understand her personal triggers and take ownership for her inactions (not demonstrating appropriate selfless giving). Seeing herself more clearly, Amber was able to empathize and behave more graciously toward her daughter in those types of moments. The result was that Amber's relationship with her daughter improved.

Using natural cleaning products is akin to taking the time to listen, assess, and evaluate your specific set of M–D Relationship Dynamics and address them with a clearer self-awareness and strategic approach in the moment.

This process of listening to, assessing, evaluating, and addressing your specific set of M–D Relationship Dynamics can be done individually or with the help of a state-licensed mental health practitioner. (See Appendix for further explanation and a list of types of clinicians.) Such clinicians can work with either an individual or with a mother and daughter together in either a clinical or consultation role. More than one method may be needed if you want to accomplish more than one goal in your M–D Relationship.

A third option for cleaning mirrors involves the use of "natural" technology-infused cloth products (microfiber-like materials) that lift dust, lint, or dirt off the mirror without redistributing it to other areas of the mirror. Relationship-wise, this is akin to simply learning how and when not to let one run-in or one source of tension affect your interactions in another arena. Many times in an M–D Relationship, either the mother or daughter will overgeneralize or project (redistribute) past assumptions, hurts, argument material, etc. onto current situations that have nothing to do with the person in front of them at that moment. Now, there are likely valid reasons for the redistribution, but it will only continue to make matters worse.

Natural technology-infused cloth products require special processes for materials to be incorporated into the cloth which results in the cloth being able to lift out the dust, lint, or dirt; these processes can be complex. Though not an exhaustive list, here are some of the situations for which you might need special processes to help you clean your Life Mirror:

- You have experienced any trauma in your life that is inhibiting your ability to connect meaningfully with others consistently.

- You have difficulty (or been told you have difficulty) in your relationship with substances or drugs.

- You have a family history of (or are currently struggling with) any degree of mental health issues like depression, anxiety, bipolar disorder, ADD/ADHD, etc.

- You have a family history of (or are currently dealing with) medical health issues.

You can work on this kind of personal cleaning individually, but depending on the complexity of your situation, the assistance of a state-licensed mental health clinician skilled in working with factors specific to your Life Mirror background would be most useful. (See Appendix for further explanation and a list of types of clinicians.)

The cleaning methods mentioned above are for those mothers and/or daughters who desire to clean their Life Mirror for *personal* clarification reasons to help improve their M–D Relationship. However, there is sometimes another reason people clean mirrors—I'll call that reason the decorative-room-enlargement-illusion effect. Such approaches can do wonders for the room in which the mirror resides. But if the home is still in disarray, what's the real gain?

Similar to the decorative-room-enlargement-illusion effect, there are times when mothers or daughters will Febreze the mess in their relationship to present to themselves and others the scent (sense) that their M–D Relationship Dynamics are better than they actually are. My hope and belief, since you are reading this book, is that you both care enough about each other not to choose this approach.

However, if you *are* currently using this approach, please know that there is no judgment here, no condemnation. I know there are life circumstances and situations that only you know and that have contributed and/or are contributing to the current pattern(s) between you and your daughter or mother. There *is* good news! Today is the day you can take your first step toward change. You can do it. I've been there. You are not alone.

VIEW FROM THE COUCH

"What did I ever do to you?" said Rebecca to her daughter, Kate. Kate replied, "*You existed!*" Kate then went on to state how she believed her mom did not want a daughter just like her but a daughter who was what she never got to be—a successful singer. This intense scene occurred in the second episode of the second season of the hit TV show *This Is Us*.

That line, "You existed," smacked me in the face as I watched the show and saw the strain and emotional turmoil that actors Mandy Moore and Chrissy Metz portrayed through their mother and daughter characters. It's a turmoil that exists—albeit to varying degrees—in *all* M–D Relationships. What struck me was the candor of the daughter's observation that her mother's very existence was the standard by which she, the daughter, judged herself and found herself lacking. Rebecca's criticism-coated compliments hit close to home for me as I recalled my early struggles as the daughter of a beautiful and talented but critical mother.

My mom was gorgeous. In pictures that I've seen of her in her prime, she was *always* impeccably dressed to the nines while flashing a coquettish smile. That was *my* mom. Even as she aged and her hair went silver-grey, her plump and peppy presence dominated any room she entered.

At first, I thought that her criticisms of my appearance were because of her concerns about the effect it might have on my being able to get hired for TV commercials and modeling gigs. It seemed that she was never satisfied with anything regarding my appearance. That dissatisfaction was the script she sprayed onto my Life Mirror in my early years.

Though some of my mom's *dissatisfaction* spray may have seeped into cracks within my Life Mirror and contributed to my drive to make a better life for myself by excelling academically and athletically,

> WMNTTD
> _____
> Most of the time, I don't see how my scripts affect you.

it did eventually morph into my own sense of determination to push myself to meet goals that I would set. My determination became to better my lot in life *and* (I hate to admit it) to feel good about myself too. (Dang it! That overcompensation thing just seemed to sneak in there.)

While in my older years I have learned the benefits of not tying your self-esteem to what you do but to who you are inside, it seems that my determination is one of several things that I have sprayed onto the Life Mirrors of my daughters' lives. It comes out in the comments or inquiries I'll make about how they are spending or not spending their time. Sometimes it's in the way I look at them—they call it my Jamaican glare—if they are not attending to something that I'm endeavoring to have them handle on their own. Through infant, toddler, tween, and now teen years, I've seen how my daughters' mirrors have been affected by the times and ways that I have sprayed my determination script in their direction.

VIEW FROM THE CHAIR

Your Sprayed Concept
Mothers need to remember that they were *first* daughters. So mothers, as a daughter having your daughter hat on, it'll be important for you to take time to consider what script(s) your mother sprayed onto your Life Mirror. Think about the (a) reactions, (b) expectations, and (c) validations that your mom did or did not have toward or of you during your early years. This is going to take some additional courage on your part to go there with me; I know. But I also know that you *do* have it in you to look long and hard at your Life Mirror regarding those script(s).

Daughters, your mother is not intentionally trying to ruin your life. She loves you in her own imperfect way. Still, her imperfections need not impede your growth and development into the (future or current) woman you see in your mirror. For you, daughter, it'll be important to take a look at the scripts your mom has sprayed onto your Life Mirror thus far. Also, ask yourself this:

- "What life circumstances may be prompting her to say or do what she's saying or doing?"

- "What is she doing that is getting on my nerves and/or is, according to her, not getting noticed by me?"

- "When was the last time I asked my mom about how her day is going and really listened to her?"

Daughters, I know it might not be an easy thing for you to do, and it's going to take courage on your part. But know that something good can result from it—even if it only reminds your mother of what it's like to be a daughter your age. It's possibly something your mom has not had time to give much thought to since birthing you.

CODE CRACKER

- What are two specific ways in which you and your mother or daughter are like each other and different from one another?

CHAPTER 13
COVER IT^{SM}

The fourth key in The Remedy is Cover It. This involves identifying, establishing, and maintaining appropriate boundaries/protections in your M–D Relationship.

I had *really* bad acne when I was a teenager. It did not help that when I was stressed or mad at someone or upset with myself, I would pick those pimples and develop scars. In the moment of picking, I would feel good. However, that good feeling was quickly followed by feelings of remorse when I'd see the pink color beneath my beautiful ebony skin.

My mother would grimace and look away with disgust and contempt whenever she saw the latest outbreak of acne on my face. Her silence was usually broken by a trickling of incessant commentary about what I was eating or not eating and about what I was wearing or not wearing—though I never understood what my clothing had to do with my face! As poor as we were, she eventually got more direct with me by addressing my facial and body acne and subsequent scarring with expenditures on makeup. Yup! She began to spend what little spare change she had on buying me makeup.

Yuk!

I *hated* makeup.

At first, my mom would cover up my facial blemishes with foundation and then plaster the beautifying makeup onto my face. I found out quickly that the process went a lot better if I didn't fuss. I *did* fuss, though, because I did not like the feelings of rejection and shame I was having on the inside of me. There was my mother covering up my face and telling me to cover up my acne-scarred body parts so that I'd appear presentable to others (the "others" being people I either knew or would potentially meet by chance in my daily travels to and from school). The last time I'd checked, there was no one of any supposed importance visiting my not-so-safe section of the South Bronx. So what was the big deal about my appearance?

That was the logic of my train of thought—the train of thought that covered up the hurt I felt inside about my appearance not being good enough even for my mother. Talk about major rejection. So I covered up my feelings by going cerebral—into my head—all logical, rational, and defensive.

Eventually, I graduated to being allowed to put on my own makeup, and thus the tradition of the daily cover-up ritual was handed down from my mom to me. With the makeup application being more in my control, though, I began to apply less and less makeup on a daily basis. The daily basis soon became "only on special occasions" or when my skin breakouts got really bad. Regardless of the occasion or situation, the idea of wearing makeup was still a sore spot for me.

Years went by, and by the time I graduated from Brown University and landed my first corporate job at a Fortune 500 company's human resource department, I at least felt some-what good about my ability to "fix my face" and not scare anyone with my appearance. In hindsight, I did not look *that* bad. I wasn't picking my skin as much, and the acne was not as prevalent. It must have been a teenage hormonal thing. However, the sore spot festered.

When my BFF hubby asked me to marry him, I was standing before him in my favorite tattered farmer-overalls outfit. I was surprised out the wazoo! I realized that someone *could* actually see my true inner beauty. The capper is that he said I was outwardly beautiful too. He expressed that he loved me for *me*. I said yes to his proposal of marriage!

The wedding was a year away. Not being an avid fan of shopping (actually, I hate shopping), I dreaded having to look for a wedding dress. Why? Because there seemed to be this underlying expectation that I would have my mother accompany me when I went to pick it out.

I'll cut to the chase: I did not have my mother accompany me to pick out my wedding dress.

Okay, you can pick your mouth up off the floor now. I had my reasons.

At the risk of sounding like I am justifying my decision, I will say this: I wanted to feel like a beautiful bride-to-be during a process that involved an activity (shopping) that I did not enjoy.

Try balancing all those internal emotions: pressure, dread, hurt, excitement, trepidation, helplessness, anger—just to name a few. The whole shopping-for-the-wedding-dress-thing was a huge struggle for me on so many levels. I desperately yet sincerely knew that I had to find a balance and an appropriate boundary that would guard the sore spot in my heart regarding my outward appearance so that I would not be deflated and embittered but joyous and excited about my upcoming nuptials. I also wanted to preserve my relationship with my mother, whom I knew would say hurtful critical things about my appearance in her attempt to "help" me choose a wedding dress. This would likely have led me to verbally express things that I'd later regret and undo the years of work I'd exerted to re-establish a loving, close(r) relationship with her.

Were my mom's feelings hurt by my decision? Yes.

Did I respectfully have her involved in other aspects of the wedding planning and wedding day ceremonies? Yes.

Was she happy? No.

Was I happy on my wedding day? Yes.

I think a bride ought to be happy on her wedding day.

VIEW FROM THE COUCH

As a daughter, it was a delicate balance to establish and maintain appropriate boundaries with my mother—the woman who carried me for nine months, gave birth to me, and decided not to throw me into a garbage can. I loved her but hated some of her behavioral tendencies toward me; I needed her but desired to be independent; I admired her but wanted to be my own person. All of these dichotomies came to a head as I prepared for my wedding day.

Back then, I could see that my mother really wanted to contribute part of herself to my wedding day, and since she was of meager financial means, she'd always talked about using her seamstress skills to make my wedding dress. However, as her eyesight and stamina diminished as she entered her early seventies, the "making of the wedding dress" became the "making of the veil," and then even that became tenuous. With the reality of her physical limitations in addition to the anticipated criticism-laden dynamics surrounding my appearance, I felt between a rock and a hard place when it came to making the best decision. Not everyone was going to be pleased. I did the best I could, but wrestling with that whole dilemma sucked bigtime.

Thinking about it now, I know that I would not make a different decision today. However, there is an ache in the pit of my stomach that makes me understand some of the anguish and pain she must have felt: seeing her baby daughter getting married and wanting to be able to give something meaningful—*something of herself*—to the occasion, but seeing her dream of making her baby daughter's wedding dress fade away. I understand now, 25 years later, how that unfulfilled dream likely left her feeling devastated in the depths of her bosom. She probably felt that she had nothing left to give to me and, by extrapolation, she was no longer of any value to me. But these were things my mother never told me.

And back then I did not have the words or wherewithal to fully share with her how I was feeling about everything either.

But you would not have known any of this was occurring within each of us on my wedding day. And when I think of *that*, I am overcome with gratitude and amazement.

The genuine graciousness with which my mom carried herself and interacted with me and my husband's family . . . my eyes are now flooded with tears just thinking about how much strength she walked in that day. It was all out of her love for me that she chose not to bring attention to herself on my wedding day (she covered all of her own pain) so that her baby daughter could shine and have center stage. That was my mom. That was *my* Trojan!

As a mother now myself, I find that it's such a delicate balance to establish and maintain appropriate boundaries with the very offspring whom I've birthed. They are separate individuals apart from me, but they are still my daughters whom I've not only nurtured but to whom I've also grown close. I have to constantly remind myself that I am first my daughters' mother, endeavoring to prepare them to be positive contributors to society. These reminders of my maternal role are particularly hard for me to adhere to when my daughters don't talk or share as much with me as I'd like. In those moments—when they go silent—I tend to start badgering them. I'm taming my instinct to badger because I've found that it comes across to them as criticism—and criticism never goes over well with my daughters.

Duh!

Ya think I'd be quick on the uptake when I see *the look*—their eyes rolled toward heaven. (Why *do* they look up to heaven anyway? Are they praying or thinking something else? If they are praying, then I sure hope they're praying *for* me instead of *about* me.)

WMNTTD
As your mom, I sometimes don't know how to feel when I see you not needing me.

I might not know if they are praying for me, but I do know what they are thinking about me during my barrage of badgering when they go silent. They're thinking, "I wish this woman would just shut up already!" How do I know what they're thinking? I know what they're thinking because I've asked them in the moment, and that is what they've told me.

Ouch!

But I'll take the hit and feel the initial pain of their truth because I am intent on them not covering up their real thoughts and feelings.

There are times when I've caught myself and stopped mid-badger to say, "Oh, I'm doing it again, aren't I?" and they slowly nod their heads with a half-smile/half-smirk on their face. Then I smile back and mimic their expression, and we all end up busting a gut with laughter.

It's taken us a long time to get to the bust-a-gut laughter moments, but I think I've gotten better over the past four years. The day is coming so quickly when they will no longer be in our home but gone off to college. Oh my! Those sixteen years snuck by. I need to continue to be present while giving them their space and enough room to decide when they want to circle back around to connect and share with me.

Each time they circle back around, though, I notice that

they are different. They are more developed in their own thoughts and reasoning. They are more opinionated, like me (a chip off the ol' block!). But the trick for me is to know when to listen and when to speak up so that they don't clam up. Note to self: Two ears and one mouth = twice as much listening as speaking.

I do enjoy seeing each of them become their own person.

VIEW FROM THE CHAIR

Within an M–D Relationship, there are times when you will need to establish appropriate boundaries and protections, especially as you delve deeper in clarifying the issues in your dynamics. You may cover up aspects of your heart or life for the sake of self-preservation so that healing can begin, continue, or be completed within yourself first and then, by extension, within your M–D Relationship. This is similar to when a stabilizer film covering is placed over a mirror's crack (before the resin is applied) to keep the separation steady just long enough for a binding adhesive substance to be applied. (This repair process was discussed in Chapter 11.)

As we have seen in Chapters 10–12, for small cracks/rifts in your M–D Relationship, the remedy involves the Face It stage where you are

- *preparing* your heart to receive and give unconditional positive regard (love) through the proverbial mirror that gets held up to you regarding your actions/inactions in the situation

- *implementing* a course of action that incorporates information that you've learned about yourself in that proverbial mirror

- *realizing* where you are both lacking in love toward each other and that any corrections will

be imperfectly perfect in light of the realizations
you've had

As you go through the Face It stage, big(ger) cracks or
relational rifts may come to the surface, necessitating the next
step in The Remedy: Clarify It. The Clarify It stage involves
addressing what has been sprayed onto your Life Mirror and
understanding, choosing, and using your different options for
cleaning off the dirt, scum, and grime. In order to do this,
though, you will need some clarity.

PSR™ CLARITY

An optimal goal for clarifying things is to get PSR Clarity
on what's been covered up at the deeper levels—below the
surface—of your M–D Relationship. Achieving PSR Clarity
involves getting a clear(er) picture of

1. **P:** a *process*

2. **S:** (your) *self*

3. **R:** your *relationship* with your mother or daughter

Process
The process for making a mirror is complicated. According
to *How It's Made*, at an industrial level the process starts with
a clear sheet of glass that goes through a number of steps
that wash, blast, scrub, polish, spray, apply, and heat various
liquefied metals (tin, silver, copper) and paints that are then
given time to cure into a reflective mirror.[24]
Similarly, your life has been a compilation of multiple
layers and agents spraying scripts of life experiences onto you
and fashioning your Life Mirror, which is what you are mirroring to your mother or daughter. The process of changing
your mind, emotions, and actions takes time and involves

- examining past and/or current dynamics within your M–D Relationship

- identifying your current thoughts/thinking patterns

- changing your individual behavior patterns

Self

In Chapter 12, you read about how you need to examine the past and current scripts that you have developed about yourself—as a daughter first and as a mother second. These scripts affect how you, as a daughter, feel about yourself. Those are the feelings that you will carry or have carried into your role as a mother.

Relationship

You will need to peel back more (onion) layers to determine what M–D Relationship patterns are playing out in your interactions with each other. These dynamic patterns fall into four categories. Let's take a look to see what dynamics may be occurring in your M–D Relationship.

The Four MDRDs™ (M–D Relationship Dynamics™)

Category 1: **Mom-In-Daughter™ (MID)**

This dynamic is where the mother sees herself *in* her daughter. This perspective affects the majority of their interactions. The daughter is an extension of the mother—her hopes, dreams, and/or anything that's unresolved for the mother. Though not limited to the sports world, I have seen and continue to see this dynamic play itself out in the work I do as a board-certified sport psychologist working with scholar-athletes.

Ann was a fifth-grade student gymnast who asked her mother, Suzanne, to take her to see a sport psychologist for performance anxiety issues. Suzanne brought Ann to see me. In gathering background information during our first session, I learned that Suzanne was a former competitive athlete who'd experienced a freak accident during a recreational activity.

Ann's maternal grandmother was a vocal presence in Suzanne's life and would not hesitate to express her strong opinions about what Suzanne should or should not do. Suzanne told me that she had purposed to take a different approach with Ann by allowing her to make decisions for herself (which resulted in Suzanne finding a sport psychologist when Ann requested to see one).

While performing an uneven bar routine, Ann had a mishap and injured herself. Though her injury healed, Ann's fears began to affect her performance in other areas. Ann's coach—a strongly opinionated woman like Suzanne's mom—continued to press Ann to "just attack" the routines. Suzanne would acquiesce to the coach's pressured directives to Ann despite seeing her daughter struggle with anxiety and fear.

Suzanne had hopes and dreams of Ann progressing to the next level beyond what she herself had attained back when she was a competitive athlete. Suzanne's identification with Ann drew Suzanne into a dynamic (with Ann's coach) that had the script of "acquiesce to strongly opinionated older women."

This grime on Suzanne's Life Mirror wound up doing Ann a disservice. Suzanne pulled her daughter out of her sessions with me when the coach stated that seeing a shrink is a waste of time. Although Suzanne said she'd given Ann independence and freedom to make her own decisions, Ann ended up acquiescing to Suzanne's decision (do you see any generational patterns being passed down here?). On the last day of our sessions, Ann told me that she was "fine," even as her countenance conveyed a look of timidity. Her timidity was vastly different from the focused and determined manner she'd had during our first meeting. My heart was saddened.

Category 2: **Mom-Out-Daughter™ (MOD)**

This dynamic is where the mother has distanced her daughter or distanced aspects of her daughter that resemble aspects of herself that she has disowned or that were rejected by her own mother.

You can see examples of this dynamic on various reality TV shows that depict two generations of women in a family—a grandmother, mother, and daughter—dealing with issues of abuse. A grandmother will dismiss the behaviors of the (abused) mother who is rejecting her daughter who reminds her of aspects of her own sordid past, thus leaving the daughter to wander in shame and self-blame.

Sherayah was a 19-year-old student who came to see me because she was having "boyfriend problems." After obtaining a background history and comprehensive assessment, I learned that Sherayah's mom was in an abusive relationship when Sherayah was young and would blame her daughter for the couple's turmoil. Sherayah often felt anxious when she was under stress and feeling alone. Her mom's frequent engagement in self-defeating interpersonal patterns with

Sherayah—blaming her for everything—would leave her feeling that she was undeserving of any attention due to the scripts her mom had sprayed about ways in which she herself was unworthy of love and attention.

Category 3: **Mom-Or-Daughter™ (MOrD)**

This dynamic is where each person in the relationship relates to the other as either a parent or a peer.

> **Parent**: This involves a symbiotic *caring* dynamic in which parent-like responsibilities are inappropriately placed on the younger of the two individuals. You will often find this dynamic occurring in families in which a mom has substance use/abuse or relationship abuse issues which leave the daughter to be the adult in the relationship.

> **Peer**: This involves a symbiotic *camaraderie* dynamic that inappropriately places relatability at the forefront of the older person's needs (for acceptance, validation, connection, non-rejecting experiences, etc.). You can find this dynamic occurring when a mother has experienced some kind of neglect, rejection, or abandonment by her family of origin or within her marriage/romantic relationship(s). Her daughter becomes a replacement/salve to escape the emotional pain or receive the validation that was lacking in her own life.

Category 4: **Mom-And-Daughter™ (ManD)**

This dynamic is where the mother sees her daughter as a separate entity/person due to the mother appreciating her own self without fearing the possibility of being hurt or rejected by her daughter's actions/inactions or by an aspect of her daughter that reminds her of herself. This is the type of dynamic that will allow each to (agape) love each other without losing aspects or a sense of themselves in the process.

View (again) from the Couch

Mothers within the M–D Relationship are going to be hurt or rejected by their daughters in some way at some point in time; it happens in varying degrees and different ways for each pairing. The old adage "Don't take it personally" is a quick reminder to mothers whose daughters are endeavoring to figure out who they are.

I recently asked my daughter Jasmine if she was enjoying this teenage time of finding herself. She looked at me as if I'd just danced in public and then sarcastically quipped, "I don't have *time* to find myself, Mother. I'm too busy trying to finish my homework at a decent hour, study for my SATs, and identify colleges to apply to." We both chuckled.

I must admit that what I *really* wanted was to know whether or not I was doing right by her and giving her enough space to find herself. Her answer, though, made me pause. Then I empathized with the reality of her world as a junior in high school. She and her sister are swamped with honors and AP classwork and figuring out junior year and beyond. When I considered all of that from her perspective, I realized that I was okay with her response, and I appreciated her candor. She was being exactly in the moment of her reality and being herself in it.

I was able to reach this realization with my daughter because of the process I've undergone to recognize where my dynamics with her had been and the personal work I've done to implement appropriate boundaries to place a protective covering over our M–D Relationship.

VIEW (AGAIN) FROM THE CHAIR

The Covering
In order for you to get (and keep) a handle on where you are in The Four MDRDs, it'll be important for you to become aware of and implement boundaries. According to Dr. Cloud and Dr. Townsend,[25] boundaries are like a property line. Property lines tell us what we are and are not responsible for, and they function to keep the good stuff in and the bad stuff out.

Boundaries are the key to you being able to develop a healthier sense of yourself so that you will be better able to get a handle on

1. where you both begin and end as individual people

2. what the specific tension points (mirror cracks) in your M–D Relationship Dynamics are

3. how to identify these tension points more clearly so that you can know when they are about to get triggered

4. what specific things you can do to address your specific personal needs first

5. what specific needs you can and cannot meet in and for your mother or daughter

6. strategies for communicating with your mother or daughter to address the tension points.

As I mentioned in Chapter 10, the process of fixing a crack in a mirror involves the use of a stabilizer that covers the crack and holds the edges together. This covering (boundary) facilitates a connection so that a binding substance can be added to the crack to repair the mirror over time. Similarly, coverings (boundaries) are important for your M–D Relationship. They provide a necessary protection so that some degree of interaction can continue (or not) and subsequent healing can occur between a mother and daughter.

If your M–D Relationship has no cracks or only small cracks, that's great. All you need to attend to is a minor fix and the splatter on your Life Mirror. But if your M–D Relationship has large cracks, then a more in-depth analysis will be needed.

Fracture (Crack) Analysis
The approach and process for fixing a cracked mirror depends on the size and age of the mirror and crack. For mirrors that have larger and deeper cracks, a more involved method of Fracture Analysis needs to be used. Fracture Analysis involves

1. collecting all the broken pieces

2. making a map of the cracks

3. finding the pattern and type of stressor(s) that were applied

4. identifying the direction of the crack (what specific part of the mirror it's affecting)

5. surmising the root cause (origin) of the crack within the shiny residue around the crack

6. reviewing what (external) processes combined with the stress

7. hypothesizing about how the breakage occurred[26]

Once an informed hypothesis is developed, then a specific multi-step strategy for remedying the situation can be implemented. An involved fracture analysis and remediation are best conducted by mirror experts. In the same way, the analysis and remediation of a significantly large crack in an M–D Relationship would be more involved and benefit from the input of licensed mental health clinicians who have more specialized training and could provide either consultation or clinical services to help with the more complex psychological, emotional, and behavioral patterns that are occurring.

Since every M–D Relationship Dynamic and each mother's and daughter's Life Mirror has varying degrees of dirt, smudges, and cracks, it would be impossible to cover every possible remedy to every possible situation in one book. However, Chapters 14 and 15 have some suggestions that comprise the fifth and final key of The Remedy—Engage It—to get you started on the road to healing your M–D Relationship.

PART 5
ENGAGE IT^{SM}
THE FIFTH KEY

*"Every person's remembering will be different.
That engagement is important, I think."*

—Christian Marclay, quoted in an
interview with *The Telegraph*
Visual Artist

MOTHER PRELUDE

The basis of all human connection and engagement is communication. All creatures communicate in some way, shape, or form. Human beings are different in that there is a plethora of interpersonal dynamics that factor into the communication equation. Succinctly put, communication involves

1. *conceiving* an idea/notion/thought/piece of information

2. *understanding* the piece(s) of information

3. *communicating* that piece of information

All forms of communication run the risk of the process not resulting in both people gaining an understanding of the other person.

The link between conceiving a thought and communicating it is the degree to which one is first able to grasp the meaning of—understand—the thought oneself. After this occurs, the thought can be communicated to another person so

> "UNDOUBTEDLY THERE ARE ALL SORTS OF LANGUAGES IN THE WORLD, YET NONE OF THEM IS WITHOUT MEANING. IF THEN I DO NOT GRASP THE MEANING OF WHAT SOMEONE IS SAYING, I AM A FOREIGNER TO THE SPEAKER, AND THE SPEAKER IS A FOREIGNER TO ME.
> —PAUL, THE APOSTLE (55 A.D.)

that, once the communication is complete, *understanding* develops between the two people. To grasp the meaning of what you are each saying, doing what follows in the next chapter will be key.

CHAPTER 14
FOR DAUGHTER'S SAKE

What is the purpose of being a mother? There are many different answers that mothers could give to that question, from "having a baby" to "raising a mini-me" to "I haven't the foggiest idea . . . it's just hard." Culture, race, family of origin, socioeconomic background, religious or spiritual traditions, and personal worldviews all influence and inform your answer to that question. There is no singular right answer.

How do you feel about having or having given birth to a little girl? *That* question is equally likely to have a number of different responses, each influenced by one's personal background. You've already read in the pages of this book the personal account of events and experiences that I had while growing up. Hopefully, it won't surprise you when I say that I was *not* excited when my BFF hubby and I found out that we were having girls.

There I was on the ultrasound table. As the technician said, "Well, Mr. and Mrs. Deering, it looks like you are having twin girls," you could've seen air simultaneously deflate from my face and fill up my husband's chest. He was *so* excited! I, on the other hand, had always thought that if I were to have children, they would be boys. I feigned a smile at the technician and said nothing. Then my husband took me out to eat at a nice restaurant—to celebrate.

During the car ride, I was quiet. All I could think about were all the ways in which I was not ready to be a mother, let alone a mother to *daughters*. I liked cars, trucks, and sports as a child. Any doll I had was one that someone had given me instead of a toy I'd actually requested. I hated shopping and did not like dresses or fancy makeup. Plus, for most of my own childhood to young adult life, I had not had a close relationship with my own mother. I did not even know how to take care of a *Black* girl's hair (let alone my own hair) without having to plunk down a chunk of change at a hairdresser's salon. Hair bills for two? Yikes!

As these thoughts raced through my mind, the waiter gave us our appetizers. My husband rambled on about his excitement, hopes, and dreams. Somewhere in there he likely said something about how he knew I'd be a great mom. I don't specifically recall what he'd said because my mind was in a haze—and I had to pee.

I excused myself from the table to go to the ladies' restroom. As I entered the stall, a lightning bolt thought shot through my head and a big Cheshire-cat-like smile came over my face. I rushed out of the restroom and eagerly sat down. My husband looked at me quizzically.

"Hun!" I said excitedly.

"Yes, dear?" he replied.

"I just figured out *one* positive thing about having girls."

"What is that?"

"I can take them to the ladies' restroom and they'll be okay." My smile was gargantuan.

That was all I thought that I, as a mother of daughters, could offer our twin girls. So whether you felt like I did back then or you were ecstatic about having a daughter, my hope is that the following suggestions for building a close(r) relationship with your daughter will be a starting point for you.

For your daughter's sake, just MOTHER her.

MIRROR HER.

The beauty of being a woman is that women are wired for social interactions. So, whether your daughter is an infant, toddler, teen, or thirty-something, face-to-face contact is key. Reflecting back to your daughter her sentiments and facial expressions or, at a minimum, conveying that you "know the feeling" she's expressed and can sympathize with or care for her is what mirroring is all about. You have to be genuine in conveying this, though. If not, you will lose currency for being allowed back into her Life Mirror.

This is particularly important when your daughter enters her tween and teenage years. It can be so easy for a mom to tune out, dismiss, and/or minimize her daughter's feelings and experiences during a developmental period that involves constant change for her. Your steady maternal presence is still the safe space your daughter will need to navigate the many other sources that are spraying scripts onto her Life Mirror.

OFFER HER.

It's a tricky adjustment for a mom when her daughter is transitioning from being a toddler to a tween. Though subtle, the shift in a daughter's autonomy is noticeable in two ways. First, your daughter's growth in autonomy will solidify her sense of competence. For girls, this is a psychological milestone that gets challenged during the middle school years. Second, this shift in your daughter's autonomy will necessitate a different approach to parenting—one of guidance and suggestions instead of orders and directives. Ordering and directing someone who is trying to figure things out is like loudly shouting "*Don't fall!*" at a novice tightrope walker as she traverses a rope under windy conditions. It is all about the presentation and timing.

An "I was wondering if you'd considered . . . ?" or a "Have you given any thought to . . . ?" or an "I'm here if you need or would like any suggestions . . ." goes much farther than a "You know, what you should do is . . ." or an "If I were you . . ." or a "When I was your age . . ." with your budding teenager or young adult or married-with-kids daughter. Offer her the gift of your input with an open hand and heart knowing that it may be rejected, tossed, or ignored. Again, that will be her autonomous choice.

THANK HER.

Why is it that some moms are always ragging on the younger generation for having a poor attitude? What does this accomplish? Your Gen X, Y, Z or Millennial daughter has a bad attitude. You rag on her to stop; she improves her attitude. Psychologists call this pattern a negative reinforcement loop: your negative comments, reactions, or behaviors are applied to elicit a pleasing behavior. The result will be a pattern in which your daughter will only improve her attitude if/when you rag on her.

Instead, take time to thank your daughter for the largest to the smallest—or most mundane—things she does that are kind, considerate, or helpful.

To moms reading this book, know that having an attitude of gratitude not just for your daughter but also toward your daughter can go a *long* way toward improving the quality of your M–D Relationship.

HEAR HER.

Ears were made for listening; hearts were made for hearing. From infancy to tween years, we mothers have asked and expected our daughters to listen to us (a.k.a. "Do what I say"). Our expectation is that, like little automatons, they will just listen and obey. Silently, though, I think moms are hoping their daughters will hear them and take to heart what they've spent time pouring into them, knowing that, on some level, they'll need that piece of instruction later in life.

Well, moms, daughters want and need to be heard, too. Time after time after time, at some point my female therapy clients will either say or convey some sentiment or story about their mother that indicated how they never felt heard by their mom. Feelings of anger, frustration, and hurt (and accompanying tears) tend to come up at those times in the session. The depth of hurt and pain is palpable, and it saddens me.

Mothers: please take time to slow your roll, pause (which may include closing your mouth for just a moment!), and hear your daughter with your heart.

As you are listening to your daughter, ask yourself, "Is what she's saying verbally lining up with what she's saying non-verbally with her eyes, head, sighs, etc.?" If you can't figure it out, then ask your daughter for clarification, get advice from a trusted friend, or seek out consultation services from a state-licensed mental health professional. Taking such time and making such an effort will reap dividends in improving the quality of your M–D Relationship.

ENGAGE HER.

Psychologists and social scientists agree that teenagers, despite their proclivity to give off the sentiment of wanting to be left alone, actually do crave connection with their parents.[27] However, it's a different kind of connection that they seek.

Teen years are replete with pressures from peers, school, and various types of social settings—all of which are pulling at a teenager to decide who they actually are. This process of identity development takes into account and builds upon earlier developmental milestones regarding autonomy, competency, and efficacy, all of which are centered on individualism and one's ability to be able not just to do something but do it well.

When the identity development process kicks in during the teen years, the "who am I" question comes to the forefront. In general, there is a rejection of that which has been mirrored to them in earlier years and a sloshing through what is being offered to and/or touted before them from current circles. (Moms, be one of those circles by being present and available to your daughters!)

What mothers sometimes lose sight of is there is also a weeding out process that is occurring within their daughters. The weeding out process is happening in the silent parts of her day when Decals of Difference are in front of her, and she has to decide for herself what her choice will be. This is the tightrope she walks daily. The internal and external pressures are so tense that you can never predict (unless it's during the monthly visit from "Aunt Flo") when she might pop a cork! This is why the thought of trying to engage with a daughter can be an excruciating and terrifying prospect to a mother.

In times like those, it'll be important for you to remember the earlier years when your daughter was not a teen and you had times of engagement with her. Think about and re-experience the feelings of enjoyment you had and/or the gleeful expressions emanating from your daughter in those moments. Those qualities still reside within your daughter—they are just buried beneath the barrage of new choices, pressures, and life situations she is currently facing.

If you as her mom can be steady, patient, and more strategic in picking the times in which to attempt to engage your daughter, your efforts will not be in vain. Additionally, keep in mind that when she was younger, you were the one who introduced different things (toys, games, books, outside activities, etc.) to her and she would engage with/in them. As she gets older, it'll be important for you to show sincere interest in and engage in the things she expresses interest in and/or brings to share with you. These new interests can become the foundation for a new common ground upon which you can work to improve the quality of your M–D Relationship.

RESPECT HER.

Despite the Queen of Soul (Aretha Franklin) being hailed as the originator of the "R-E-S-P-E-C-T" sentiment within women's circles, the song was actually written by a man—Otis Redding—about his desire for respect from the significant woman in his life. Similarly, a mother's role as a parent would be expected to elicit the same deference from her daughter. "Give me some respect here, daughter. After all, I carried you for nine months and birthed you." This seems reasonable, right, moms? Definitely.

What mothers can lose sight of, though, is that daughters are worthy of respect too. Respect is an action of deference you give to someone whom you believe is important and worthy of your considering their rights and preferences in your decisions and actions. Well-intentioned mothers have been respecting their daughters from the beginning by caring for their own bodies while pregnant, finding the right medical professional to help with delivery, feeding, clothing, changing diapers, and doing all those things mothers do when daughters are really young and dependent on them.

When it comes to respect, the key differentiator here is the *dependent* factor. For the most part, a well-intentioned

WMNTTD
As your mom, it's hard for me to see you as your own person apart from me.

159

mother desires that her daughter will not hang on to her apron strings indefinitely. The Western European-influenced ethos of expectation in American society is that daughters will become independent at some point in time. With that in mind, it is important for mothers to parent while keeping in mind that one mothering goal is to raise an independent daughter, to the degree that such a goal is culturally salient for them and their family.

Mothers need to *re-spect* (look again upon; give particular attention to) their daughters and realize that they are going through a growth process that the mothers themselves underwent. Granted, you may not agree with all that your daughter is deciding to do. Remember, though, that she is way younger than you are. If you cannot respect her for slogging her way through the tough maturation process of trying to figure it all out, then at bare minimum respect the process that she is undertaking. But at a maximum, respect your daughter.

VIEW FROM THE COUCH

As a mother myself, I think about my mom and how she MOTHERed me. I see how, for the longest time, my Life Mirror had sprays of scripts that neither said much about me as a person nor accurately reflected me—my heart, interests, desires, and passions. That's not to say I was unaware of the things I liked or disliked or what was in my heart to pursue. It was just that my awareness was smeared with the soap scum of my mother's relationship and familial disappointments and sprayed with the toothpaste splatter of her encounters with racism for being Black in America.

Despite that residue, her Life Mirror did reflect the value and importance of hard work and determination despite difficulties. Her life also mirrored to me a predilection for tasteful, high-quality items. (I think my tasteful eye is genetic because, despite my frugal ways, my daughters have the same eye for well-made, pricey items that I've not let them act on. We'll have to see what happens when they start living on their own.)

When I look back, I see that my mother really "had it going on." I did not realize the magnitude of that until I graduated from college and had to begin the process of getting my own thing "going on." I guess, though, she never got to the place of appreciating that I, her daughter, did have it going on way before college graduation—it was just a different kind of going on than she was used to.

It would have been nice if she could've appreciated that aspect of me more. I needed her to MOTHER me, for daughter's sake.

CODE CRACKER

- As a daughter, what aspect of your MOTHER do you feel you need the most today?

DAUGHTER PRELUDE

"The song is first of all about self-acceptance—mainly for young women and women in general. There are so many expectations placed on us . . . women on a daily basis—whether it's the way we look, the way we dress, what size we need to be, what color we should be—all these expectations and all these molds we have to fit into or that we think we need to fit into. Oftentimes, because of this, we feel we need to go through all these extremes to love ourselves . . . whether it's altering our bodies, doing things to ourselves, and scarring the 'beautiful' that we already have in order to feel beautiful. And I think that's so false and so twisted, and I wanted to make a song to remind everybody that the world needs to change their minds about you but you don't need to change for the world, because you are beautiful." [28]

—Alessia Cara
Singer/Songwriter

Since your mother did not give birth to junk, the best thing for you to do is be her DAUGHTER, for mother's sake.

CHAPTER 15
FOR MOTHER'S SAKE

DO YOU.

"I've gotta be me!" The old Frank Sinatra anthem of individuality for his day—can you hear it? Not quite? That's okay. That's a classic (a.k.a. very old) song. That's why Alessia Cara's *Scars To Your Beautiful* song is so poignant. It's specific to the life of young girls, young ladies, and women of all ages—daughters.

Because of the suffrage movement and the women's movement, there are so many more choices that young girls have today about their future. Access to the good ol' boys' network systems is now a reality. Heck, women have established their own networks that are powerful and influential not only in academic fields but also the STEM, corporate, entertainment, and athletic fields.

Whether it's Katharine Graham becoming the first female Fortune 500 company CEO; or Shonda Rhimes becoming the first female creator, head writer, executive producer, and lead executive producer of several hit primetime TV drama series; or Katherine Johnson making brilliant mathematical contributions to the first launching of U.S. astronauts into space; or Becky Hammond becoming the first female NBA coach; or Sarah Thomas becoming the first female NFL referee; or Dr. Jen Welter becoming the first female NFL football coach; or Condoleezza Rice and Darla Moore enjoying their golf tee-time at Augusta National Golf Club—these are prime examples of daughters (young ladies and women) cracking the bastions of race- and/or male-dominated fields with their feminine presence. These women did all these things by working hard and just being themselves.

But—*news flash!*—you are not here on this planet to be those women. Their path in life is already taken. You, however, have a specific path in life that can only be filled by you being uniquely you!

You did not birth yourself; your mother birthed you. Because your mother birthed you and did not birth herself, she cannot be you—and you cannot be her. That's not your role; that's not your calling.

Your role or calling is to find your own path and be who you are. That is the greatest compliment you can ever give your mother: to grow into the person you are.

ASK HER.

Have you ever noted the feeling you get when someone asks you for your advice? Your attention zeroes in, you consider your words, and you endeavor to share your advice in an attempt to be of help to the person who asked for your input. Then, when that person takes your advice and it actually helps them, have you ever noticed what you feel then? Usually, it's some sense of fulfillment and satisfaction that your input was valued, appreciated, heeded, and helpful.

Well, that is what your mother likely experiences when you ask her for her input or advice. You see, mothers spend most of the early years of the M–D Relationship telling, instructing, and directing their daughters in what to do. They do this without having the time or luxury (given everything they are juggling) to explain themselves or their reasons for why they say what they say or do what they do.

When you were a teenager, maybe your mother tried to interject such background information into conversations, but she may have had to do so in age-appropriate ways. As you get older, though, the notion of her daughter going out into the "big 'bad' world" gets any well-intentioned mother concerned about her daughter being prepared and informed about those other facts of life that she thinks will be of help to you.

Some mothers have difficulty holding their tongue, and they may come across as bossy or nosey, interjecting their opinions and viewpoints in ways that are overbearing or off-putting to their daughters. When this happens, there are some daughters who'll just tune out their mother or be selective about what they do and don't share with her.

Our youngest daughter got that way for a period of time regarding anything related to academics. I had a tendency to jump right in and share my helpful strategies with her, and she would get quiet. When I finally figured out how to give her what she really wanted—for me to listen and hear her and not give advice—she began to ask me for my input.

For me, as a daughter, my mother was so critical and opinionated that it got to the point where I did not even tell her I was dating anyone until I'd gotten engaged to my BFF hubby. Seriously! I kid you not. I still loved my mom, though, despite all of her critical ways.

When I finally arranged for her to take a trip to Boston to stay with me so she could meet my fiancé, I was determined not to argue with her about anything she could possibly think of to criticize about him (where he lived, what he did for a living, etc.). All three of us went out for lunch in Brookline, MA. We ate, talked, and entertained her questions—to which all of my BFF fiancé's responses were spot-on. When he dropped me and my mother off at my apartment, the silence between the two of us was deafening. Still, I simply went about the rest of the day intent on catering to whatever she needed to make her stay comfortable in my small abode.

As evening rolled around and my mom ate the modest meal I'd made for her, she conspicuously cleared her throat. I nonchalantly continued eating. She cleared her throat again.

"Yes?" I replied.

"Well," she said, looking at me with a sideward glance, "aren't you going to ask me what I think?" I paused. I did not know what to say. She'd always told me that if you don't have anything good to say, don't say anything. In this situation, though, I felt I was doomed if I said something and doomed if I did not say anything. Why did she want me to ask her anything, on this day of all days?

So, not knowing what to say that would be truly honest but not spark an argument, I replied, "No. But if you'd like to share your opinion, you may."

My mom straightened her posture in her seat, positioned her neck just so with her chin stuck out just so, cleared her throat, and pronounced, "I have nothing to negative to say."

Well, *that* was a first!

I felt as if someone had just knocked me over in my chair. Then I felt my mouth form a small grin. She looked back at her food and resumed eating.

At that moment, a few thoughts collided in my head: (a) I was glad I told her my honest answer—that I did not want to know what she thought—and yet I still invited her to share her opinion; (b) I was glad she shared her opinion with me because it let me know where she stood on the subject of my intentions to marry my BFF fiancé; (c) if that wasn't a stamp of approval, I don't know what was   but I still would've married him if she'd had negative things to say.

I confess that is the opinionated, passionate, confident side of me that had to take a stand against my mother's way of seeing things and take ownership for my decisions separate from her. I would've understood her concerns if I had not looked for the qualities she'd raised me to look for in a husband: "someone who loves you, is hard-working, and a DLE (doctor, lawyer, or engineer)." I'd internalized them on some level, with the first two qualities factoring into my decision to get engaged.

Ten months after that lunch, my BFF hubby and I got married in July. It was a great day!

In September, I called my mom to tell her that my BFF hubby and I were doing well, to thank her for always praying for me and asking God to give me a good man, and to thank her for participating in my wedding and sewing the lovely knickknacks for me. I told her that I loved her and that we'd talk again.

A month later, my mother died unexpectedly—the day before my birthday.

I would never be able to ask her any more questions. *Ever.*

UNDERSTAND HER.

There's an old Jewish proverb that says "Wisdom builds a house, but understanding furnishes it." Understanding requires that the two people who are involved in the communication process not only listen to each other but also hear each other and walk away from the encounter with a new appreciation of each other.

As with furnishing any home, each piece of furniture has a purpose and a function; it has a fit and a place within which its use will be maximized based on the intent, need, and desire of the homeowner. The piece of furniture that I've referenced a lot in this book is a mirror. A mirror's purpose and function are mostly to provide a reflection that informs us about ourselves and/or enhances the perceived dimensions of a room.

In your relationship with your mom, there have likely been and will be times when she does things that you don't understand, that will seem or feel unfair, or that will be flat-out wrong. If you take the time now to honestly look at yourself in the mirror, you have to admit that you have probably done the same and come across to your mom that way.

I'm not saying that you are your mom; you're not. What I am saying is if you can take a moment to realize that the reasons you have for thinking she does not understand you may be the very same reasons she feels that you don't understand her. You are both expressing it differently based on each of your personal experiences.

With that in mind, I can assure you that, on some deeper level, your mother would really appreciate your understanding. Understanding of what, you may ask? Well, understanding that she has sacrificed and continues to sacrifice a lot for you out of the love she has for you.

This is not intended to be a guilt-trip statement but a reality-check point for you to consider. Here are just a few things to remember:

- Provided you are not currently grounded for anything, the freedoms you enjoy are freedoms she once had and, if married, chose to share with her significant other (your progenitor).

- If she is not/no longer married, she chose to give up those freedoms on an even deeper level (to have raised or still be raising you all by herself).

- With the arrival of her bundle of blessing—you— she had to further divvy up her time, energy, and resources and balance everything to keep it together on the home front and work front, if she works out-side the home.

Toss in sleepless nights, morning sickness, taking you to the doctor and playdates, laundry, homework (hopefully she is not doing yours for you), and hormonal changes. The good, the bad, the ugly—all that she does she does for you out of that maternal love that commits to being there for you no matter what. It is all this, and then some, that your mom would really appreciate that you understand about her.

GIVE TO HER.

Mothers give so much that they get to a place where they don't know how to receive (help, praise, honor, etc.) from others, let alone the loved ones whom they birthed. Dr. Gary Chapman wrote a book called *The Five Love Languages*.[29] Initially, it was for married couples, but his research then began to expand to other members within the family unit: namely, children.[30] As a daughter, it would help your M–D Relationship if you would determine what your mother's love language is and endeavor to give love to her in the language that best speaks to her.

I know that one of my main love languages is quality time. After making a concerted effort to spend time with one of our daughters, Jasmine, doing things she likes to do, I am now finding that she takes the time to watch football games with me, which is something I like to do. I know that she has never read Dr. Chapman's book, so I don't think this new addition to our M–D Relationship was purposeful on her part. However, I know that if you look to see how your mom attempts to connect with you, this will give you some insight into her love language. People usually reach out to others in the way that they would like others to reach out to them. Sounds a little like the Golden Rule, doesn't it?

You can even take this one step further and know that if you try to reach out and give to your mom in the way you would like to be reached out and given to yourself, you might increase the likelihood of finding new ground upon which to improve your M–D Relationship.

HUMOR HER.

Okay, so I'm not suggesting that you quit your job or throw out your sense of sensibilities and become a comedian for your mom or manipulatively keep things light when you're around her. That would suggest that you should be disingenuous, and that would not help any kind of relationship, let alone an M–D Relationship.

What I am suggesting is that you keep in mind that laughter is medicine for the soul. Now, this may be hard for those whose temperaments are on the melancholy or phlegmatic side. However, making an attempt to see the humor in things (without being insensitive to someone's feelings) can go a long way toward improving the dynamics of your M–D Relationship. The best place to start using humor is on yourself.

Lighten up! Yes, I did say lighten up. I see you starting to grin. I'm not crazy. Okay, maybe you do think I am crazy.

I hear you thinking, "How can you possibly be suggesting that I lighten up? Don't you know how toxic or overbearing or intrusive or . . . or . . . What would ever make you think that it's possible for me to inject humor into my interpersonal interactions with my mom? You have no idea what my mom's like. You've not had to live with her."

Well, you're right on all fronts—except one. I have many reasons to think that it's possible for you to inject humor into your relationship with your mother. Here's a question: if you don't currently have humor in your repertoire and your M–D Relationship is strained, would your adding the ability to laugh at yourself (not your mom) or see the humor in situations pertaining to you help you relax more? If your answer is no, then I'd ask you to consider if your current serious/tense demeanor is helping your M–D Relationship situation at all. If the answer is still no, then what would you have to lose by changing things up a little?

While research by NIH indicated "little evidence for unique positive effects of humor and laughter on health-related variables," it also indicated that "there are no negative side-effects . . . and [humor and laughter] can be used . . . to help reduce stress and improve healing."[31]

THANK HER.

In Chapter 14, I encouraged your mom to thank you. The reason I did this is I know that you as a daughter genuinely love her and care about her on some level and are trying or really have tried to "do right" by her. If you're a teenager reading this book, I know that you have attempted to help around the house or tried to be nice to your siblings, at least some of the time. If you are an older daughter, I know that you have tried to include your mother in aspects of your life and probably even sucked it up for the sake of "making her happy just this once" to keep the peace. Those are not small things, and she ought to express some thanks to you for at least trying.

Similarly, I know that your mom in her own imperfect way has tried to do things for you, and, for the most part, it comes from a place of love for you as her daughter. So she might be rough-around-the-edges in her adeptness regarding her execution of the deed, but her intentions were at least heading in the well-intentioned direction. Again, she is not perfect (she never will be). But neither are you perfect (or ever will be). If you can at least see that you both are imperfectly trying to do perfectly without perfect success, then maybe you can tell her thank you—for the little and large things—with some regularity (not just on Mother's Day).

Having an attitude of gratitude will go a long way toward firming up the foundation upon which you'll be able to (re) build your M–D Relationship. Don't wait until you yourself become a mother to have such epiphanies about the kind of mother you have.

I want to pause here for a second to speak to those of you whose mothers were, for lack of a better descriptor, not the most desirable: those mothers who have either abused substances or you through harsh words, emotional manipulation, abject neglect, or violence of any kind. Words on a page cannot begin to express how much my heart hurts for you and the possible void that is lingering there in your heart and spirit to have a mom or have your mom be a mom to you. Please know that anything that I've written so far is in no way meant to imply or suggest that you are responsible at all for her choices in life.

Let me say it again: you are *not* responsible for your mother's choices. For her not to see the precious gem you are is a very sad state of things, not just for you, but for her because she has missed out on a lot.

I am also not suggesting to you that you are to continue in or enable behavior or interpersonal dynamics that are not healthy or respectful of your personhood or life. I trust that whatever boundaries you have established are there because you've deemed them necessary and appropriate. If you have not established or you find it hard to establish such appropriate boundaries, do consider finding a competent and appropriate state-licensed clinician (psychologist, licensed clinical social worker, or licensed marriage and family therapist) who can join with you to help you through your particular situation.

My hope is that at some point in your lifetime you will be able to give thanks for the experiences you've had and see them as situations that have shaped and molded you into the beautiful diamond you are.

Be thankful . . . anyhow.

ENGAGE HER.

The well-intentioned mom wants to respect her daughter's space as she gets older. This is a hard transition for mothers to make, given their natural inclination to be nurturers and dyadic relational beings. From the time you were born, your mom has been pouring into you (hopefully, positively) physically, mentally, emotionally, and spiritually. She has also been the receptacle (holder) of aspects of you that you may not be aware of—like your hopes, dreams, hurts, etc. Her adjustment to your growth and expanding life circles can take some time.

It is during this adjustment time when many mothers start to question their usefulness to you, their daughters. They've invested so much of themselves, and they want to make sure you're okay—all the time! But deep down, whether or not they want to admit it, they know that they cannot assure that you'll be okay all the time. So the need for connecting with you somehow starts to grow within her heart and emotions.

The way in which you both navigated and negotiated the closeness/separateness/push-pull dynamics inherent in an M–D Relationship is going to influence things for you as a daughter. In a nutshell, if your mother has not had great personal experiences of being separated from others or has found it hard to allow you to be/become your own independent person, the process for you to engage with her will be trickier than for someone with a mom who has not had such experiences or difficulties.

I recently spoke with a client who, with her teen daughter present, stated that her daughter had anxiety issues. As she talked to me, the teenager was physically clinging to her mother, and the mother was not setting appropriate boundaries during their interactions. I surmised that when it came time for the daughter to go away to school (if she actually went away), this mother would find it hard to be separated. At the same time, if the daughter did not address the root of her anxiety, she would have a hard time finding ways to engage with her mother as a young adult lady in the future.

To engage your mother, it'll be important for you as her daughter to establish what your parameters will be for the interaction. Ask yourself this: What aspects of your interaction with your mom can you tolerate, which do you have trouble tolerating, and which can you not tolerate at all? For each aspect of tolerance, specify a minimum and maximum time limit for such interactions. Also think about what interests, activities, hobbies, and proclivities you share with your mom and seek out venues or events where you can spend time with each other in such activities. Then speak with your mother about the options that exist for you to spend time with each other. Once you are with her, employing some of the DAUGHTER strategies will prove helpful in improving the foundation of your M–D Relationship.

RESPECT HER.

It is not uncommon for daughters to idolize their well-intentioned mothers early on in their relationship. They literally look up to their mothers. They hang on her every word. This lasts from birth—until age two. Then a daughter undergoes a process in which she ventures away from the safe space of her mother to discover different things about herself. Somewhere during that process (unless it is specifically addressed early on), daughters can lose a degree of respect for their mothers.

That loss of respect can be communicated from the blatant vent of "I hate you" to the subtler displays of toddlers and tweens talking back to their mothers, calling them names,

> **WMNTTD**
>
> ---
>
> As your mom, I feel hurt when I don't experience you valuing who I am.

"play" slapping them, and throwing mini-fits of defiance in their mothers' presence. Loss of respect for moms can also come across in a daughter having and/or expressing sentiments that convey that her mother is an entity who's there to do the daughter's bidding. Such behaviors occur to varying degrees.

As a daughter, you may want to give some consideration to something I mentioned back in Chapter 14: well-intentioned mothers have been respecting their daughters—treating them as important—from the beginning in numerous ways. Your mother birthed you and thus has the title of *mother*. At the bare minimum, her title deserves deference. My hope, though, is that she is more than a title to you, that she is someone for whom you have some love and affection. I believe this about you because you have been reading this book to find ways to improve and deepen your M–D Relationship.

Respect, then, is something that will speak volumes to your mother and begin to assuage any past or existing rifts in your M–D Relationship. Here are some ways you can respect your mom:

- Compliment her when she does anything well or if she has put herself together nicely.

- Praise her, privately and in public, for her positive qualities and personal contributions to yourself and/ or others.

- Acknowledge her expertise when you find yourself needing input on a topic she may have experience with (and which you'll have gained more information about having already Asked her)

- Address her in a manner and tone that conveys that she is valuable as a person.

View from the Couch

It seems like daughters have to do way more than mothers to lay a foundation for improved M–D Relationship Dynamics. I never liked that part of the process as my mother's daughter. "Why do *I* have to bend? Why do *I* have to compromise?" is what I used to think. That is until I realized that bending did not imply weakness or surrender.

Bending actually requires strength, strength that I needed to admit that I did not have in and of myself. I needed divine help with that. Bending also meant that I had to have definitive boundaries around my sense of self so that I would internally know how far a bend was possible for me so that I did not snap or break. Breaking would not do me or anyone else any good, now would it?

As for compromise, I realized that *com* (to bring together) and *promise* (a type of oath) would require two people agreeing to a type of promise that would bring them together. How can two people walk together unless they agree? Agreement is key. If that does not exist, then the result will be a win-lose situation. How conducive to fostering M–D Relationship depth and closeness would it be if either my mom or I (or my daughters or I) was often on the losing end of things? That, to me, would only breed resentment and be fodder for further contention.

My stepsiblings likely wrestled with these dynamics with our mother. From my vantage point, it seemed to me that they were constantly bending and compromising aspects of themselves in their relationship with our mom. One even went into debt to appease our mother's desire for the flashy and glamorous things in life. My half-siblings' efforts to experience the glitz were not sustainable. In my estimation, that was not an optimal situation; it only exploded when our mother died unexpectedly. I don't know if it left them with any sense of closure. I hope they have the kind of closure they need.

I know I have.

CODE CRACKER

- As a mother, what aspects of your DAUGHTER do you feel you need the most today?

SECTION THREE
THE REWARD

CHAPTER 16
THE TRIFECTA REWARDS

My heart is so full of excitement and joy for you! You've come so far not only in reading this book but also in taking on board some of the considerations that I've presented to you along the way. Do know that as you laughed, chuckled, felt your heart tugged, or even cried, my heart has been with you in each moment? "How can that be?" you might be wondering. Well, although I might not have had the exact experiences that you've had, the feelings we share are universal. Pain. Joy. Sadness. Anger. Happiness.[32]

So *many* emotions! It's as if we were pregnant all over again. *Yikes!* (Disclaimer—no, I'm definitely not pregnant again. If you are, congrats! But you get my point, right?) The rewards for undergoing the process you're undertaking far outweigh the risks you've taken to address The Rifts in your M–D Relationship. I call them the TriFecta Rewards:

1. Closure

2. Closeness

3. Collaboration

GOOD THINGS COME IN THREES

Although I list the TriFecta Rewards in the order above, I will discuss them in reverse order in the following three sections.

Collaboration

On the point of collaboration, well, my mom and I never quite got to that point given her unexpected death. However, with my own daughters, a new rhythm started to take shape during their sophomore year of high school. They seemed to "get it" that I was actually for them and not out to nag them. (How did that happen? Here's the secret—I stopped nagging and started listening more with a heart to hear them.)

I've found that when I feel like I'm about to pop, I stop and ask myself three things:

1. "What am I feeling?"

2. "What is *really* making me feel this way?"

3. "Will the next words out of my mouth spray stuff on her or communicate that I'm paying attention to her?"

The result has been that we are open to taking another's being into consideration in an understanding way, which informs how we go about doing things together, being together, in our M–D Relationship.

Closeness

I was recently in the car with my BFF hubby and daughters, Jasmine and Candace. We were heading home from the movie theater yapping about our favorite parts of the movie and what rating (out of ten) we'd given it. The subject meandered on over to the topic of my not being into the mystery novel genre and their penchant for it, which led to the topic of traveling across the country and abroad.

Our youngest daughter, Jasmine, then piped up about her interest in West Coast colleges, and my husband and I joked with her about our plans to travel once they both headed off to college. In the midst of the playful ribbing and chuckling, my husband and I informed them that most dormitories close for the holidays. What followed shocked me.

The millisecond of silence—between our statement and Jasmine's question, "So what am I going to do during the holidays if I'm out West?"—was as fast as the resounding clang was loud when the dime dropped for her, and she exclaimed, "How much *is* a plane ticket?"

To this, I quipped under my breath but loud enough for her to hear, "You *may* want to consider that when choosing a college."

Before I knew it, my joking around slipped into a realm of maternal sentiments that I *never* thought I'd hear myself feel, let alone say:

- "You can come home to visit." (What I'd wanted to say was "We'll pay for your ticket." But I didn't want to influence her planning or decisions.)

- "When you come home, please do your own laundry." (They both replied, "We do our own laundry now!" Good. They didn't know I'd really felt like saying "I'll do your laundry" but caught myself. *Whew!*).

- "You'll call, right?" (That was nice and neutral.) "Every week, right?" (Dang it, I let that one slip! Uh oh . . .)

- "You know, in-state tuition is *way* cheaper."
- "You *will* come home to visit, won't you?"
- "You can FaceTime me too, you know." (Long pause. Was that my heart feeling something?)
- "I'm gonna miss you girls." (Wait, that was a tear creeping down the corner of my eye.)
- "I'm gonna miss you girls *a lot!*" (I'm actually feeling sad at the thought.)

For the next few minutes, both our daughters had to remind me that they were still high school juniors. But it was too late; I'd gone there—to the realm of feeling the hole of their not being with me in our home where I could hear their voices, interact with them, hear about their day and how they are doing, feed them food, and the like.

When I wiped away my tears—yup, they were in full flow!—I settled down and then relished the fact that I have a meaningful relationship with both of them. We are not just biologically connected but emotionally connected. Is it perfect? No, because none of us is perfect. But we are perfectly walking in our imperfections toward the goal of building our relationship with each other. There is a beauty—a *closeness*—in the mundane, the struggles, the Misses that come with the M–D Relationship.

Closure

For me (and, I dare say, for you too), that closeness can only get on the right track toward fruition when closure occurs first.

What do I mean by closure? I mean when a mother or daughter has

- faced herself in her own Life Mirror
- gone through the process of clarifying what things have been sprayed upon her Life Mirror and

hindered her from seeing herself (and her daughter or mother) more clearly

Only after completing these two steps will you be able to cover—put new boundaries around—your M–D Relationship more appropriately. In doing so, the soil of the newly enclosed common ground and the seed of the both of you within that soil will be able to grow with the nurture and attention you will both be better able to give.

When I was at Brown University, I met a kind elderly woman whom all the students called Ma Jackson. She was as fierce in her commitment to living a life of love as she was in her determination to make sure no college student she encountered went back to campus on an empty stomach. I can still smell the savory aroma of her cooking. Ma Jackson was an angel in my life not just because her Sunday meals saved me from what The Ratty (cafeteria) offered on campus but mostly for the wisdom she fed me from her PHD (Praying Heaven Down) accounts of the various life situations she had experienced.

It was Ma Jackson who—after hearing my 19-year-old frustrated and whiny self bellyache for three hours about how much of a "pain in the butt my mom was" and how "unfair my mom was" and "how critical she was of me"—looked at me with her big eyes and said, "Daughter, you will only ever have one mom. *Love* her."

For a long time, I'd thought that to love my mom meant to make her happy, give in to doing what she wanted me to do, not argue with her (she was old, after all), spend money on her, etc. etc. etc. However, what I learned pretty quickly was that to love my mom meant something different:

- It meant to respect and honor her in a way that took into account where *I* began and ended and where *she* began and ended—a way that respected the mental, emotional, and physical boundaries that were in place at any given point of any given day of our interactions.

- I was *not* responsible for her happiness; she was.

- I *was* responsible for interacting with my mom in a way that did not flaunt or take for granted my mom's responsibility for herself.

- I was responsible for looking for ways to express my heart of love toward her (whether in kind or thoughtful deeds or expressions that I knew she would like). If I could not provide something materially, then I could love her with whatever nonmaterial things I could provide.

This process was a trial-and-error one for me. The key was that I committed to doing things differently in light of Ma Jackson's timely counsel.

Her counsel was timely in two ways.

This was the first time someone had said something to me that was so true that it hurt, but it was said with so much love that it did not hurt at the same time. My decision at that moment—committing to act differently with my mom—was an internal shift that I knew I would need some kind of divine help to implement. Eight years after that moment, I got married. Two months after that I had a regular loving conversation with my mom and told her "I love you," and one month after that I received the unexpected phone call informing me of her sudden death.

Although we were devastated by the news, the ensuing drama with Lil and Debra showed me point blank what it's like when daughters don't have closure with their mother. I wish I'd had more time with my mom for her to continue to interact with me in the new married stage of my life. But I would not change a single thing that transpired during those eight years of me loving on my mom.

The second reason Ma Jackson's counsel was timely was that it was a seed that got planted in me and inspired me to become a psychologist. It gave me a living example of how someone can be present with a person when they are emotionally and mentally raw and vulnerable. In love, they can speak that which needs to be said in that particular moment, knowing that it will likely hurt the person—and not hurt all at the same time.

Ma Jackson would always give me one of those *huge* hugs that would squish my face as it got lost in her big arms. I can still feel the love, acceptance, and warmth of her presence.

I offer you a similar virtual big hug as I wish for you the closure and closeness that *will* result as you implement the ideas and changes that have occurred within you as you've read this book.

Things *will* be different. Things *can* be tweaked. There *is* hope.

Carolyn

Carolyn was in her 50s, a divorced working mother of a young adult daughter and son. She came to see me at my private practice to help her deal with significant bouts of insomnia. During my initial assessment, the first several meetings, Carolyn shared her background story—including her childhood with an alcoholic and abusive father and an enabling mother. Though her children were young adults, her son lived with her while her daughter had moved out and hardly ever communicated with her, which was distressing for Carolyn.

Over the course of the next ten months, I worked with Carolyn to help her look in her Life Mirror and identify her current view of herself and the scripts that had been sprayed on it. I then helped her process how those sprayings were affecting herself, her dynamics with her children (her daughter, specifically), and her health.

Through a holistic mind-body-spirit therapy approach, Carolyn was able to make the shift from a woman who saw herself as a wet kitten to one who saw herself as a lioness who is capable of being not only protective but also caring, compassionate, and communicative. Supportively, I worked with her on how to implement aspects of this newfound insight, and soon she was able to find ways to reconnect and engage with her daughter.

VIEW FROM THE CHAIR

At the time that I was meeting with Carolyn, our daughters were younger than they are now. Since I did not have young adult children, I relied not only upon the compassion that I had (and still have) for those who are hurting but also upon my clinical training and work with numerous young adult and college-age students, in particular young adult daughters who have shared intimate details of their hearts with me regarding the rifts in their M–D relationships.

In my work with these daughters, I have succeeded in providing them with what my colleagues who, like me, adhere to Attachment Theory call a "corrective experience."[33] I became that mirror for them that showed what their mothers were not able to so that their daughters could get rejuvenated and inspired to re-engage with their mothers in a more optimal way. Nothing excites me more than when my clients have lightbulb moments that spark them toward action to make changes in their lives that connect them to themselves, others, and their life goals.

That's my heart. That's my passion. I'm here to help.

VIEW FROM THE COUCH

Rather than endeavor to "take the speck out of other's eyes" while I have a "plank in my own eye," I have also worked on myself by looking into my Life Mirror and addressing the planks in my eye as it pertains to my M–D Relationships. It has not been an easy process, but it has been rewarding. Weeping endured for *many* nights, but the joy that has come in the morning is something that I would not trade for anything in the world.

For me, that joy comes from knowing that, despite *all* my imperfections, I am continuing to be myself with my twin daughters. They are seeing me:

- own up to my shortcomings, which involves specifically apologizing to them.

- stand with my arms wide open to provide them with a safe place to run back to.

- get up again and again when their teenage ways knock me back to the reality of what effect my actions or inactions can have on them.

The other day, one of my daughters, Jasmine, came home from school, plopped down in my home office, and began telling me about her day. I didn't need to give much prompting. The conversation just flowed. She laughed, I laughed. She giggled, I giggled. I gave my usual response, to which she added my typical mannerisms (mimicking me quite well), which made us both bust a gut.

She even mentioned an idea about a homework assignment, and instead of my just spouting my opinions about it, I asked her if she wanted to hear my input. Turns out, she'd already thought of my idea but said she was still open to hearing what I was thinking. It was a precious time together. I so enjoy her company.

A few hours later, Candace came home from her after-school activity. I could see that she was tired from biking home and her long day. She moved around the house going from one of her potted plants to the next, watering them, as she told me about her day. I knew I had only a few moments before she went upstairs to do her homework, so I started to remind her of my upcoming business trip. When I conveyed the information, she looked right at me with a face that looked like she'd been jolted with electricity as she exclaimed, "No one tells me *anything* around here!" I then reminded her about how she often gets when she has a lot of work to do and that no one can talk to her because of her gruff vibe.

I mirrored to her what the family experiences when she gets that way—and even modeled using humor while doing it!—and I spoke the truth to her. We both chuckled, and I gave her more details about my business trip. Though short, the time we spent in that interaction was also precious to me; it almost seemed like she was going to miss me while I was gone on my trip. (Note to self: I need to find more creative ways to connect with Candace during her seasons of busyness.)

Mothers and daughters are always a work in progress.

Epilogue:
The Letters

LETTER TO MY BFF HUBBY

First, I want to thank you for being exactly who you are and not trying to be someone that you're not. Your kind and gentle manner and conscientious effort to hear and listen to me and consider and take in my input have always made me know that I have an open door with you.

I knew it was scary for you to propose to me as the thought of taking on the responsibility of caring for another person's life was daunting for you. But from the get-go, you have jumped with your whole being (not just both feet) into this thing called married life with me. Though I think that sometimes I have been a handful, it is your love—expressed in your consistent and steady patience with me—that has been a balm for so much healing in my life.

You protect me with prayer and your presence and provide for me in your persistent pursuit of God's will for your life, our marriage, and our family. You also provide in your steadfast faithfulness to meet the many challenges of the day in your chosen career and workplace as you seek to do right by your clients, extend mercy with those who are difficult to deal with, and walk humbly before your ultimate boss, God Himself. Your integrity shores up the steady foundation of your life of honest living, which is the bedrock of our marriage and family. You work tirelessly and faithfully—at much cost to your physical, mental, and emotional stamina—so much so that I get concerned about your longevity. But then I have to trust God that He who brought you into my life will super-naturally sustain you so that our years together will continue to be long, rich, and full.

You are a rich man indeed. Though Clarence in *It's a Wonderful Life* said that such wealth is because a man has many friends, I would disagree. Your wealth is in the many seeds of hope, faith, encouragement, and loyal support and belief in me and our daughters that you plant each and every day in the consistent commitment and determination you exhibit by going to battle for your family—in your prayer closet and at work—to ensure that we have that which we need. And in the midst of it all, you *still* manage to be present for me and our daughters each and every day, and that includes weekends.

With all our imperfections, you continue to perfectly walk with the integrity and honesty of a man who knows that his life matters both in the greater scheme and the minutia that makes up our life together.

My warrior. My Spartan. My hero—I sing your praises because I am a woman so blessed by you being a man, a real man, my man—a beautiful, intelligent, strong, Black, God-fearing, and godly man of wisdom, love, and strength.

Thank you for choosing me to be your wife.

With much respect for you, and always honored to be

Your Helpmate, BFF, and Well-kept Rose,
Michelle

LETTER TO MY DAUGHTERS

My hope is that after you've read this book I've written, you will have a better understanding of who I am, where I've been, and why I do things the way I do.

I know that I've said a lot of things to you over the course of your lifetimes so far. However, there are many things that I've not said to you yet. Here are the big ones:

- Congratulations on attaining your post-secondary and graduate academic degrees.

- God bless you and your marriage to _____ (insert name of the nice, God-fearing, godly young man who also fits the rest of the special criteria that you know about, *wink wink*).

- Congratulations when you give birth to your own children.

Still, the things I've never told you as of your 16th year of life have to do with your father, my BFF hubby.

But first, let me share some words with you that I've held onto for a while:

1. Judge a man by what he does, not just what he says. If his actions don't consistently line up with what he's saying, then toss him to the curb.

2. Take your time to observe a man when he is with you and especially attend to his reputation when he is not in your company. How he reacts and responds to different and stressful situations will give you insight into how he will react and respond to you.

3. Align with a man who fully supports and believes in your dreams and aspirations. Your role as a helpmate to him does not start until *after* he's put a ring on it and said "I do."

4. Trust is earned. If it's broken, then it'll take exponential means for it to be earned back again. So don't skip having a man earn your trust, especially when considering marriage.

Why am I talking to you about marriage? Because I believe the type and quality of life that you'll have in the future—and the type of mother you will grow into—is linked to the type and quality of the man you marry.

Why am I saying that to you? Well, as you already know, I was raised by my mom, your grandmother, who was a single mom. Granted, she was a single mom by necessity and choice, having escaped from an abusive marital situation. Being a single mom by any circumstance is a *hard* life. Single moms have the sole responsibility for being both mother and father to their child. No matter how well they balance or attempt to exemplify that to their children, it is an insurmountable task for a single mom to be all things to each child.

There are specific perspectives and life experiences that a well-meaning, good husband/father brings to the life of his child, in particular to his daughter. Those aspects of a dad are crucial to a daughter's sense of herself as a young lady who is becoming a woman. Within the marital union of a man and woman, the husband demonstrates a sacrificial giving of himself that seeks to protect and provide for his wife in an honoring, supportive, non-domineering, and loving way. He sets the tone in collaborating with his wife and incorporating her input. He facilitates and nurtures confidence within his daughter by showing her how he does so with his wife, and he conveys the mechanics of how his daughter can navigate the systemic male-dominated world with cunning and prowess. He takes on the load of providing this kind of safety structure for his wife and, by extension, his daughter.

As you well know, I did not grow up in that kind of two-parent family household. But you have. I believe your blessing was the result of God's grace and your maternal and paternal grandparents' prayers. That being said, what I've never told you is that I sometimes feel that you take your father for granted, and that ought not to be so.

I'm not saying you've been outright, maliciously disrespectful to him. What I am saying is that due to my lack of experience—not being raised by my biological father—I've not always been the best reflection of what it means for a wife to respect her husband. I've been walking in circumstantial ignorance for over 25 years.

You've likely seen the outworking of this in my passionate side, voicing my opinions in most circumstances, but that is because your father has given me the freedom to do so in our relationship, knowing that I grew up not having the opportunity to express myself or my opinions. So, while you might think that I wear the pants in the family, the reality is that your father really *does* wear the pants in the family. I've just not conveyed that to him in a way that speaks unconditional respect, which is a man's real love language.[34]

There was something my mother, your maternal grandmother, once told me. She said, "Even if you don't like a person, you need to show respect for their position." She mentioned this to me early on in my career in corporate America at a Fortune 500 company.

With regards to your father, my BFF hubby, I know that you like him. What's there not to like? He has a dry wit and sense of humor that always gets a smile or chuckle or an "Honestly, Daaaa*duh*!" response out of you no matter what kind of day you've been having. He always listens to you and takes your thoughts and feelings into consideration all the time. He respects and encourages you to express your opinion. He tirelessly—even when he is doggone tired—helps you with anything (especially techy stuff) that is causing you difficulty. He has communicated and continues to communicate to you his unwavering belief in you and your ability to "do anything you put your mind to." He spends time with you in your world (watching TV, reading books, and going to movies) and yet gives you space to be your own persons who have their own likes and dislikes. He speaks the truth in love to you and shares his heart hopes for you and your future. He has even agreed not to kill (*heh heh*) the first guy who seeks to date one of you, giving the lad a chance to make a case for himself as to why he should have permission to share your company. Such a man—such a father—is worthy of unconditional respect from you (and me), *always*!

The quality of the man you marry will affect the quality of life you end up having. My life is all the richer—not in terms of money but in terms of the prosperity I have in peace, safety, and security—for having my life intertwined with his. He sharpens me, respects me and my integrity, challenges me, and inspires me, all in the way he lives his life and walks in an understanding way with me. He (agape) loves me in his actions, not just his words.

Does he have issues and shortcomings? Yes. But because he acknowledges his deeds (good and bad) as "filthy rags," puts his trust in God's provision for salvation (John 3:16), and daily recognizes "from whence cometh his help," he has walked and continues to walk in an understanding way with me in love. In all of my own shortcomings, I am a way better mother to you because of your father, my BFF hubby, being in my life.

It is my hope and prayer that both of you will marry men just like your (earthly) father.

Love you both,
Mom

LETTER TO SINGLE MOTHERS

Dear Awesome Mother,

I am writing to you because I am the daughter of a single mother. My hope is that, in the preceding pages, you have found some solace, validation, or hope. I thank you from the bottom of my heart for buying and reading this book. On the off chance that you have not gotten anything from this book that is beneficial to you and your particular situation, I wanted to share some things with you that I hope, if you have a daughter, you will hear as if she herself were saying "What A Daughter Never Tells Her (Single) Mother."

First, **I watch you**. I watch you when you are with me and even when you are not with me because your presence permeates my world.

Second, **I fear you**. I fear (am afraid of you) because I see the strength you possess to plug away day after day through the tough situation you are in, and I know that strength could easily be used to "pop me one" if I ever were to downplay your struggle. There is some veracity to the saying that you "brought me into this world, and you can take me out."

Third, **I fear you**. I fear (revere you) because I see your resolve to provide despite whatever you may or may not think you are able to do. You are *big* in my world: the world you are making for me and training me up to encounter in your *big* way.

Fourth, **I need you**. I need you because you are my world, my sustenance. What you do impacts me, and I need you to have a positive impact on me.

Fifth, **I respect you**. I respect you (whether or not I may like you or how you tend to treat me) because you respected me enough to give birth to me. So, because you are and always will be my mother, I give you my respect.

Sixth, **I crave your tender side and need your tough side**. I crave your tenderness because being raised by a single mom is tough on a daughter who has to face the world starting with a "without dad" label on her. That lack hurts and needs your tenderness to help me not beat up on myself; I can't even imagine how the hurt affects you. I need your toughness to help guide me through the outside systems that I face. I want to face them with the toughness you exhibit daily as you provide for me.

Seventh, **I love you**. However imperfectly—amidst my silent treatments, sighs, shouts, tears, and challenges, I love you and always will because you're my mom.

With much admiration and respect for you and all you do,
Sincerely,
Daughter of a Single Mom

ACKNOWLEDGEMENTS

To my Father: Thank you for life, for always knowing my heart to be of help to others, and for making a way for me to do that.

To my BFF Hubby: Thank you for loving me and for your unwavering belief in and unconditional support of me and my dreams.

To my "Bright Eyes": Your depth and quiet, reflective manner are unique and special to me. "Quiet waters run deep." I love you *and* your depths.

To my "Smiley": Your candor, passion, and laughter are just a few of the many gifts you possess. You have a good and giving heart, and I love you.

To my Chip: Thank you for 20 years, two months, and five days of your friendly, accepting, caring, and humorous feline companionship that has always meant the world to me. I miss you terribly, my booby, but I'm glad you're with your brother eating out of *his* heavenly bowl.

To my Daisy: Your absence is deeply felt, but memories of you are forever imprinted; you taught me persistence. I will miss our lap times.

To Victoria: You're a godsend. Thank you for always being in my corner—through everything.

To Jennifer, Lisa, and Ojochide: Thank you for your friendship, sisterhood, input, and selfless giving. You continue to make the Body real to me.

To Kary Oberbrunner (my baldheaded publisher and "brother" with a girl's name): Thank you for being obedient to the call on your life to start and establish Author Academy Elite, for being a servant who gives and leads by example, and for believing in me and my vision for the writing within me.

To Abigail Young (my editor and "angel" at Stressless Edits): Thank you for your enthusiasm, support, and encouragement as you midwifed the birthing of this book, my "baby."

To Debbie O'Byrne (designer at JetLaunch): I am so grateful for you and your open heart that "got me" from the beginning. You take the art of listening and creating to a new level.

To Chris O'Byrne (president of JetLaunch): You take service to a whole new level. Thank you for your support and attention to the details.

To Debra Matthias and Chris Borja (two of the nicest, most kindhearted, and giving folks I know): Thank you for being you. I'm so glad that our paths have connected.

To Jim Akers: Thank you for walking in integrity and with a sincere heart, and thank you for your support.

To the Ladies of WPN (Women's Power Networking): Y'all rock it each and every day. You continue to inspire, challenge, and change me—for the better—from the inside out.

To the Players on the Stage of My Life: Though I don't have all the answers to the "whys," I am grateful for what has been sprayed and how it's shaped who I see in my Life Mirror today.

APPENDIX

TYPES OF STATE-LICENSED MENTAL HEALTH CLINICIANS

Psychologist—PhD, PsyD, EdD

Psychologists attend graduate school and study psychology. The American Psychological Association recognizes the doctoral degree as the minimum educational requirement for psychologists; these degrees include the PhD (Doctor of Philosophy), PsyD (Doctor of Psychology), or EdD (Doctor of Education). Graduate training focuses on all aspects of human behavior, with an emphasis on research and scientific methods.

Training for the PhD, PsyD, and EdD typically includes 4–6 years of academic and clinical preparation followed by 1–2 years (ranging from 1,500 to 6,000 hours, depending on the state) of full-time supervised clinical work with patients in addition to national licensing examinations and state jurisprudence examinations.

Some states require that they also regularly complete state-mandated continuing education credits/hours after licensure. Psychologists have the requisite training to provide clinical ("talk therapy," cognitive-behavioral therapy, EMDR therapy, etc.) or consultation services for normal to complex issues.[35]

Psychiatrist—MD

Psychiatrists attend medical school and earn an MD (Doctor of Medicine) or DO (Doctor of Osteopathic Medicine) degree. Beyond the four years of medical school, they can take additional specialized training in psychiatry during a residency (an additional 3–4 years). Training for psychiatrists focuses primarily on biological aspects of mental illness. Because of their medical training, psychiatrists can prescribe medications, and their work with clients may or may not include talk therapy combined with medication management.[36]

Therapist—LCSW

Social workers attend graduate school and study social work, earning an MSW (Master of Social Work) degree, and may or may not go further to obtain state licensure as an LCSW (Licensed Clinical Social Worker). Training typically includes two years of coursework and practical experience working at agencies in the community; licensure requires an additional 3,000 hours of supervision, which may or may not involve clinical therapy work.

Social workers are trained to perform psychotherapy with a particular emphasis on connecting people with the community and support services available there. Those clinicians who have a master's degree (or doctorate) in social work can only advertise their clinical services as a therapist or psychotherapist or psychoanalyst but not as a psychologist because they have not fulfilled state licensure requirements in order to call themselves psychologists.[37]

Family Therapist—LMFT

Marriage and family therapists (MFTs) are mental health professionals who earned a master's degree or PhD in marriage and family therapy from an accredited graduate school and have undergone training in psychotherapy and family systems. Graduates are taught to address mental/emotional issues using treatments that focus on the mechanics of relationships as they pertain to a marriage, family unit, and/or other group.

Licensure requirements vary from state to state but generally involve obtaining at least 1,000 hours of supervised clinical practice and scoring successfully on the National Certification Examination.[38] Those clinicians who have a doctorate in MFT can only advertise their clinical services as a therapist or psychotherapist or psychoanalyst but not as a psychologist because they have not fulfilled state licensure requirements in order to call themselves psychologists.

Counselor—LPC or LMHC

LPCs (Licensed Professional Counselors) and LMHCs (Licensed Mental Health Clinicians) have, at a minimum, earned a master's degree in counseling from a nationally or regionally accredited institution of higher education and completed a minimum of 3,000 hours of post-master's degree supervised clinical experience within two years. They must regularly complete state-mandated continuing education credits/hours after obtaining licensure and pass the National Counselor Examination (NCE) or a similar state-recognized exam.

The nature of an LPC's clinical training varies and depends upon the clinician. Those clinicians who have a doctorate in psychology (PhD, PsyD, or EdD) but who advertise their clinical services as an LPC or LMHC have not fulfilled state licensure requirements in order to call themselves psychologists.[39]

ENDNOTES

1. Shrier, Diane K., Tompsett, M., and Shrier, L. A. (2004). Adult Mother–Daughter Relationships: A Review of the Theoretical and Research Literature. *Journal of the American Academy of Psychoanalysis and Dynamic Psychiatry, 32*(1), 91–115.

   Boyd, C. J. (1989). Mothers and Daughters: A Discussion of Theory and Research. *Journal of Marriage and Family,* 51(2), May, 291-301. Retrieved from: http://www.jstor.org/stable/352493

2. Kinsella, M. T. and Monk, C. (2009). Impact of Maternal Stress, Depression & Anxiety on Fetal Neurobehavioral Development. *Clinical Obstetrics and Gynecology, 52*(3), September, 425—440.

   National Research Council (US) and Institute of Medicine (US). (2004). *Children's health, the nation's wealth: Assessing and Improving Child Health.* Washington, DC: National Academies Press. Retrieved from: https://www.ncbi.nlm.nih.gov/books/NBK92200/

   Saint-Laurent, R. and Bird, S. (2015). Somatic Experiencing: How Trauma Can Be Overcome. *Psychology Today.* Retrieved from: www.psychologytoday.com/blog/the-intelligent-divorce/201503/somatic-experiencing

3. Comas-Diaz, L., Luthar, S. S., Maddi, S. R., O'Neill, H. K., Saakvitne, K. W., and Tedeschi, R. G. (n.d.). The road to resilience. Washington, DC: American Psychological Association. Retrieved from: www.apa.org/helpcenter/road-resilience.aspx

4. Boyd, C. J. (1989). Mothers and Daughters: A Discussion of Theory and Research. *Journal of Marriage and Family,*

51(2), May, 291-301. Retrieved from: http://www.jstor.org/stable/352493

5. Cook, G. (2103). The Moral Life of Babies. *Scientific America*. Retrieved from: www.scientificamerican.com/article/the-moral-life-of-babies/

6. Piaget, J. and Cook, M.T. (1952). *The Origins of Intelligence in Children*. New York, NY: International University Press.

   McLeod, S. A. (2015). Jean Piaget. Retrieved from: www.simplypsychology.org/piaget.html

7. Saint-Laurent, R. and Bird, S. (2015). Somatic Experiencing: How Trauma Can Be Overcome. *Psychology Today*. Retrieved from: www.psychologytoday.com/blog/the-intelligent-divorce/201503/somatic-experiencing

   Comas-Diaz, L., Luthar, S. S., Maddi, S. R., O'Neill, H. K., Saakvitne, K. W., and Tedeschi, R. G. (n.d.). The road to resilience. Washington, DC: American Psychological Association. Retrieved from: www.apa.org/helpcenter/road-resilience.aspx

8. Tatum, B. D. (1992). Learning about Racism: The Application of Racial Identity Development Theory in the Classroom. *Harvard Educational Review, 62*(1), Spring, 1—24.

9. Schnall, M. (2013). "Interview with Eve Ensler: In The Body of the World. *The Huffington Post*. Retrieved from: www.huffingtonpost.com/marianne-schnall/interview-with-eve-ensler_b_3166274.html.

10. Pew Research Center (2015). *Family Support in Graying Societies: How Americans, Germans and Italians Are Coping with an Aging Population*. (May). Retrieved from: www.pewsocialtrends.org/2015/05/21/4-caring-for-aging-parents/

11. Brazelton, T. B. (1992). *Touchpoints: Your Child's Emotional and Behavioral Development*. Addison-Wesley Publishing Company: Boston, MA.

12. Chegg Inc. (n.d.). *Maslow's Hierarchy of Needs*. Retrieved from: www.chegg.com/homework-help/definitions/maslows-hierarchy-of-needs-13

13. Erikson, E. H. (1963). *Childhood and Society* (2nd ed). New York: W.W. Norton & Company.

14. Bowlby, J. (1969). *Attachment and Loss: Volume 1—Attachment* (2nd ed). New York City, NY: Tavistock Institute of Human Relations.

    Bojczyk, K. E., Tara J. Lehan, T. J., McWey, L. M., Melson, G. F., and Kaufman, D. R. (2011). Mothers' and their adult daughters' perceptions of their relationship. *Journal of Family Issues, 32*(4), pp. 452—481.

15. Eye Movement Desensitization and Reprocessing (EMDR) therapy is an integrative psychotherapy approach that has been extensively researched and proven effective for the treatment of trauma. EMDR is a set of standardized protocols that incorporates elements from many different treatment approaches. Scientific research has established EMDR as effective for post-traumatic stress in addition to panic attacks, disturbing memories, performance anxiety, phobias, stress reduction, and sexual and physical abuse. For more information, visit https://emdria.site-ym.com/?page=emdr_therapy

16. Covey, S. R. (1998). *The 7 Habits of Highly Effective Families.* New York City, NY: St. Martin's Griffin.

17. Sullivan, C. (2013). *The Clarity Principle: How Great Leaders Make the Most Important Decision in Business (and What Happens When They Don't).* Hoboken, New Jersey: Jossey-Bass.

18. Onayli, S. and Erdur-Baker, O. (2013). Mother-daughter Relationship and Daughter's Self Esteem. From The 3rd World Conference on Psychology, Counseling and Guidance, WCPCG-2012. *Procedia-Social and Behavioral Sciences, 84*, 327—331. Retrieved from:https://doi.org/10.1016/j.sbspro.2013.06.560

    Ruebush, K. W. (1994). The Mother-Daughter Relationship and Psychological Separation in Adolescence. *Journal of Research on Adolescence, 4*(3), 439—451. Retrieved from http://dx.doi.org/10.1207/s15327795jra0403_5

19. Glass Doctor (2017). *Cracked Mirror Repair.* Retrieved from: www.glassdoctor.com/content/cracked-mirror-repair

    Angel Gilding (n.d.). *Re-silvering old mirrors.* Retrieved from: www.angelgilding.com/re-silvering-old-mirrors

20. Barash, S. S. (2010). *You're Grounded Forever...But First, Let's Go Shopping: The Challenges Mothers Face with Their Daughters and Ten Timely Solutions.* New York City, NY: St. Martin's Press.

21. Bowlby, J. (1969). *Attachment and Loss: Volume 1—Attachment* (2nd ed). New York City, NY: Tavistock Institute of Human Relations.

22. Barash, S. S. (2010). *You're Grounded Forever...But First, Let's Go Shopping: The Challenges Mothers Face with Their Daughters and Ten Timely Solutions.* New York City, NY: St. Martin's Press.

23. Parris, L. (2017). *What Chemicals Are in Windex?* Retrieved from: www.hunker.com/12155369/what-chemicals-are-in-windex

24. How It's Made. (2008, November 17). *Mirrors—how it's made.* Retrieved from: www.youtube.com/watch?v=u03S1Nmslw4

25. Cloud, J. and Townsend, J. (1992). *Boundaries: When to Say Yes, How to Say No to Take Control of Your Life.* Grand Rapids, MI: Zondervan.

26. Ono, Toshihiko and Allaire, R. A. (2004). Fracture Analysis, a Basic Tool to Solve Breakage Issues. *Technical Information Paper.* Corning. Retrieved from: www.corning.com/media/worldwide/cdt/documents/2_TIP_201.pdf

27. Erikson, E. H. (1963). *Childhood and Society* (2nd ed). New York: W.W. Norton & Company.

28. The View. (2016, August 8). Alessia Cara Talks Meaning Behind 'Scars To Your Beautiful', Self Acceptance, More. [Partial transcription of interview by Author, Dr. Deering] Retrieved from: https://youtu.be/V7fTnLF8nhI

29. Chapman, G. (1995). *The Five Love Languages.* Chicago, IL: Moody Publishers.

30. Chapman, G. and Campbell, R. (1997). *The Five Love Languages of Children.* Chicago, IL: Moody Publishers.

31. Strean, W.B. (2009). Laughter prescription. *Canadian Family Physician*, 55(10), October, 965-967.

32. Ekman, P. (1999). Basic emotions. In T. Dieglesh and M. Power, *Handbook of Cognition and Emotion* (pp. 45 – 60). Hoboken, NJ: John Wiley & Sons, Ltd. Retrieved from:

https://www.paulekman.com/wp-content/uploads/2013/07/Basic-Emotions.pdf

33. Bowlby, J. (1969). *Attachment and Loss: Volume 1—Attachment* (2nd ed). New York City, NY: Tavistock Institute of Human Relations.

34. Eggerichs, E. (2004). *Love & Respect: The Love She Most Desires; The Respect He Desperately Needs.* Nashville, TN: Thomas Nelson.

35. American Psychological Association | Society of Clinical Psychology. (n.d.). *What Is the Difference Between Psychologists, Psychiatrists, and Social Workers?* Retrieved from: http://www.div12.org/sites/default/files/DifferencesBetweenDisciplines.pdf.

36. Ibid.

37. Ibid.

38. licensed marriage and family therapist. (n.d.) *Mosby's Medical Dictionary, 8th edition.* (2009). Retrieved from: https://medical-dictionary.thefreedictionary.com/licensed+marriage+and+family+therapist.

39. American Counseling Association. (2011). *Who are Licensed Professional Counselors?* Retrieved from: https://www.counseling.org/PublicPolicy/WhoAreLPCs.pdf

ABOUT THE AUTHOR

Dr. Michelle Deering helps the disconnected Rebuild, Restore, and Renew™ connections to themselves and others so they can reach their personal, professional, and peak performance goals. Through her writing, speaking, consulting, and psychological services, she helps individuals and organizations face their current situations, clarify their goals, and engage in strategic action to improve their lives.

Michelle struggled making connections with others and finding her true passion. As a young child, she suffered sexual, physical, and emotional abuse. Today, as a transformed woman, Michelle invests her time in helping others see their true reflection in their Life Mirror and equipping them to courageously pursue their dreams.

She is the founder and CEO of **Curative Connections**, a premier consulting company offering keynote speaking, consultation, and sport psychology services. Dr. Deering earned her B.A. degree in biology from Brown University, M. Ed. degree from Cambridge College, and her doctoral degree in counseling psychology from Rutgers University. She is a North Carolina and New Jersey state-**licensed clinical psychologist** and a **board-certified sport psychologist** through the American Board of Sport Psychology. She has advanced training in trauma treatment and is both a Certified EMDR

(Eye Movement Desensitization Reprocessing) Therapist and an Approved EMDR Consultant through the EMDR International Association.

Michelle and her husband, Scott, are parents of twin daughters and live outside The Research Triangle in North Carolina.

To connect, visit: www.CurativeConnections.com

Continue the process . . .

Get

THE *Life Mirror* REMEDY^{SM}

See yourself **clearer**.

Get support.

<u>Experience</u> the <u>change!</u>

DON'T MISS OUT!

Bring Dr. Deering to Your
School, Business, or Organization

AUTHOR, SPEAKER, PSYCHOLOGIST, CONNECTOR

Michelle knows the importance of bringing in the right speaker and trainer for your team.
Set the stage for success with an engaging and authentic speaker who will instruct and inspire your audience toward change. Michelle customizes each message and training to achieve and exceed the objectives of her clients.

CPSIA information can be obtained
at www.ICGtesting.com
Printed in the USA
LVOW10*0024120418
573142LV00001B/1/P